Event
Planning
Made Easy

Event Planning Made Easy

7 Simple Steps to Making Your Business or Private Event a Huge Success—from the Industry's Top Event Planners

Paulette Wolf
Jodi Wolf

with Donielle Levine

McGraw-Hill
New York   Chicago   San Francisco
Lisbon   London   Madrid   Mexico City
Milan   New Delhi   San Juan   Seoul
Singapore   Sydney   Toronto

The McGraw·Hill Companies

9 10 11 12 13 14 15 16 17 18 19 DOC/DOC 1 5 4 3 2 1

ISBN 0-07-144653-2

This publication is designed to provide accurate and authoritative information in regard to the subject matter covered. It is sold with the understanding that neither the author nor the publisher is engaged in rendering legal, accounting, or other professional service. If legal advice or other expert assistance is required, the services of a competent professional person should be sought.

—*From a Declaration of Principles jointly adopted by a Committee of the American Bar Association and a Committee of Publishers*

McGraw-Hill books are available at special quantity discounts to use as premiums and sales promotions, or for use in corporate training programs. For more information, please write to the Director of Special Sales, McGraw-Hill, 2 Penn Plaza, New York, NY 10121-2298. Or contact your local bookstore.

Library of Congress Cataloging-in-Publication Data

Wolf, Paulette.
    Event planning made easy : 7 simple steps to making your business or private event a huge success / from the industry's top event planners, Paulette Wolf and Jodi Wolf.
        p.   cm.
    Includes index.
    ISBN 0-07-144653-2 (alk. paper)
    1. Special events—Planning.   2. Meetings—Planning.   I. Wolf, Jodi.   II. Title.

GT3405.W64 2005
    394.2—dc22   2005000203

Since Paulette is never good at these kinds of things,
this dedication falls in my lap.

To Mom, Paulette Wolf
&
To Dad, Larry Wolf

In life, we are lucky to find one person who we truly admire, so I am doubly lucky
to have both of you. In my life there is no one who has had more of an influence
on who I am and who I want to be. Thank you for being such incredible
teachers and motivators and for always making sure I found my way.
I love you both!

And in loving/living memory of
Gram, Sera Fritkin

Thank you for always being our rock—strong, resilient,
and loving unconditionally. You were and always will be our inspiration.

Contents

Preface

We always love to check out the latest party book. That heavy, substantial hardback with the fabulous four-color photograph on the cover; going through pages and pages of gorgeous flowers, beautiful food stations, and fun decor—it's always a blast. Planning special events can be a uniquely creative process, one that professionals rush to get started. Choosing the color palate, the texture of the linens, the menu (the dessert!), and the flowers—other than getting to know our clients, this is usually our favorite part. Entertaining and party books are always inspirational, even if sometimes we find what *not* to do. When opening that book for the first time, it's like getting a clear picture of the author's style. We all have one. After doing a few events yourself, you're bound to find that you have one, even if you weren't looking.

For almost 35 years, Paulette Wolf Events & Entertainment (PWEE) has been planning special events. Creating a successful event is both an art and a science—one that requires meshing creativity with knowledge. Based on PWEE's experience in blending art and science to produce virtually thousands of events over a 30-year period, we have developed a set of guidelines that we always follow, and now we are giving them to you.

Having a fabulous idea is useless if you don't have the ability to execute it. A visual artist understands this principle, knowing that historic perspective, experience, and inspiration all contribute to a successful body of work.

The same principle applies to producing events. Creativity is part and parcel of a successful event, yet the "science" involved in that execution—the expertise, experience, dedication to hard work, good staff, and sound communications skills—is what separate the novices from the pros.

As the company that pioneered professional event management as it is practiced today, PWEE has learned from producing virtually thousands of special events over the last 35 years that pulling off a successful event requires meticulous preparation, a pursuit of flawless execution, and an ability to respond as a cohesive team when the unexpected inevitably surfaces. Successful events are in the details. We've produced a ton of events, but they are never the same. Quite the opposite, each one is unique in so many ways. The trained, experienced eye, however, can detect that one-of-a-kind fingerprint of a PWEE party. Sometimes it's the abundance of valet staff (we *hate* it when we have to wait forever for the car), the linens are always to the floor, and we even went through a stage where we tied the linens around the table legs. Whatever we're into at the time, that's what is projected. Whether it's chocolate browns from five years ago or colorful plaids from two years ago, draped fabrics, deep dahlias, food stations or French service, pear and brie quesadillas, or Bananas Foster (that never goes out of style), event design is a collaboration. We work with our clients and vendors to create a vision of what the party is going to feel, sound, taste, and look like.

But what if you don't have a trained eye? What if you're a novice or somebody who has committed himself or herself to a chairperson position or host position? What do you do? Almost any event book will be filled with magnificent and inspirational photographs (ours included), but what do you need to do *before* you find your inspiration? How do you achieve your vision? What are the guidelines to successful event planning? It begins with what every professional does, almost on a subconscious level, when approaching a new event. We all ask ourselves the six essential questions—who, what, when, where, why, and how? In this process we're putting together the preliminary to-do list *before* we can come up with the *real* to-do list. The preliminary to-do list is what you will need to do before you can begin to really plan your event.

Enjoy!

Acknowledgments
(with a Million Thanks)

The creation of this book has been an incredible journey and learning experience for us. Event planning is all about the details and what takes place behind the scenes. This page is in honor of all those who are backstage with us.

It started with Chris Ruys, our publicist, placing an article in *Today's Chicago Woman*, which connected us to our agent, Scott Mendel. Scott followed his instinct and championed this project. Thank you Scott for making this possible. At McGraw-Hill, it was Donya Dickerson who was so excited about this project that she made it fun. Donya, thank you for making this endeavor such a pleasure. And thanks to Eileen Lamadore, Beth Tarson, Daina Penikas, and Maureen Harper at McGraw-Hill for helping us with the process.

Daily we are so lucky to collaborate with the incredible team that we do, allowing our company to continue producing successful events. Thank you to our working family whose efforts have made this book a reality, who continually support us and make even the craziest of ideas happen: Donielle Levine for writing this so eloquently; Adam Lombardo and Erin Johnson for tolerating the last minute craziness of meeting our deadlines; Jon Kirsch, Mark Liberman, Jimmy Petrakis, Mike Bonner, Mark Kishbaugh, Scott Redding, and Gene Dibble. Also thank you to Donna Flake and Bob Sullivan for always watching the money, and Aron Levine for always watching Donielle. And to our fearless allies and collaborators: Nick Galatte, Preston Bailey, Jerry Sibal, Raymond Joseph, John Calihan, John Rent,

Jay Liberman, Lanie Hartman, John Reilly, Tim Vieira, Milan Vujic, and Ken Ryan. Thank you for never saying no and for always going above and beyond.

Marilyn Malkin, thank you for your honesty, insight and your tremendous support. Thank you Larry Wolf for encouraging us to be pioneers and helping us every step of the way. Last, but certainly not least, we need to thank Ron Fritkin, for your love, support, terrible sense of humor, and for always watching our backs.

1

Step One:
Determine the Five *W*s
and, Always, *How*

Putting together a fabulous event is a creative process with a distinct practical foundation. Who, what, when, where, why, and how? In journalism, writers are taught to include the most important information in the first paragraph of their story. Thus, when you read an article in the newspaper, you'll get the five *W*s and *sometimes how* right at the start.

Special events work in the same way. Before it's time to put together and produce an event, we need to contemplate the five *W*s and *how*. We refer to them as the event elements, and the *how*—as in "How much is the budget?"—is not just sometimes; it's *always*. As you begin to plan your event, the *who, what, when, where, why,* and *how*—your event essentials—are the foundation for your success.

Before you begin the production process of event planning, there are essential questions—the five *W*s and *how*—to answer to set the stage for brainstorming next steps.

- *Who are your guests?* How many people are you expecting? Knowing who your guests are plays a part in how you will design your event. From the entertainment to the decor, knowing your audience helps you to choose how your event will look, what kind of entertainment will be appropriate, and in some instances the timing of the event. Knowing the approximate number of guests also will dictate the location, so this is a critical question to get answered right away.

- *What is your event?* The answer to this great question will give you some insight on how to style the event. Some events, such as a company picnic, call for an outdoor location with a casual atmosphere. Some events, such as a conference, need lots of meeting room, a large ballroom, and a business atmosphere. For every type of event, there is an ideal location and environment.
- *When is your event?* This is actually a question that may not have an answer right away. Sometimes determining the time or year or specific date is part of the production process.
- *Where is your event?* Nine times out of ten, our clients come to us looking for help in finding a location for their event. If you don't know the location for your event yet, that's okay. Not knowing for sure where the event will be held is quite normal and usually is part of a normal production timeline.
- *Why is this event happening?* Having the answer to this question will help you to focus on the purpose of the event, which then gives you direction on how to spend the budget, where to put the emphasis of the party, and when it comes time, where to trim the spending.
- *How much money is in the budget?* Do you have a budget? For most people who are just starting to plan events, determining a budget can be the hardest part. After all, if you don't know how much things cost, how can you put together a budget? We help you with that later in this book, but there is one thing you can do: Figure out how much you can spend. Everyone has a bottom line that they cannot cross. Recognizing what your maximum spend is can be the best guideline.

2

Getting a grasp on these preliminary areas will steer you through the process of planning a successful event. As part of the production process, you'll need to make choices for the timing and location of your event (Chapter 2), budgeting your event (Chapter 3), designing your event and formulating the guest experience (Chapter 4), planning the menu and choosing entertainment (Chapter 5), and finally, staffing your event (Chapter 6).

It's easy in event planning to get caught up in the details of your party. Each element seems to make or break your event, and knowing where to draw the line can be blurry, even for the seasoned professional. However, if you have a firm idea of your five *W*s and *how,* you sometimes can make difficult choices (such as where to cut your budget, whether you should have live entertainment, or how much to spend on giveaways) easier because you'll know who your guests are, why your event is happening, and how much money you really have to spend. Put some real thought into these answers because they can be your map for success. With each of the following questions, you'll get answers that have direct implications on the production of your event.

Who

Who are your guests? This is a loaded question. There are a lot of things to know about your guests, and each factor has direct implications for your event options.

- *Age group.* When choosing the type of entertainment at your event, you'll want to consider the general age of your guests. For example, a jazz trio won't necessarily work at a teenage birthday party or a company picnic, and on the other hand, a disco cover band won't go over well at a seventy-fifth birthday party or corporate product launch. The same theory works for incidental entertainment as well. One extreme example is a balloon artist or a face painter. These types of incidental entertainers are best with a young crowd. An older version of these things is a henna tattoo artist or a temporary tattoo artist. These are "grown up" versions of the face painter, and adults enjoy them as much as younger kids.
- *Couples or singles.* Whether your guests come with dates or on their own also will play a big part in the types of entertainment that you have at your event and the timing of your event. If your guests are primarily singles (or people attending on their own), you'll want to avoid a dance band. When we have events where the crowd is primarily single, we like to have lots of interactive entertainment. We find that conversation and fun come easier when there are lots of activities and things to do. If your event is made up of mostly couples, then a dance band is a wonderful idea. When doing the timing for your event, you don't want too much downtime when you have mostly singles. Try food stations to spark conversation rather than a long sit-down dinner. Conversely, a long sit-down dinner is great for couples because it gives them downtime to make conversation.
- *Families.* As we discussed earlier in reference to age group, entertainment choices are based greatly on age group. A guest list that includes primarily families should have an entertainment roster that will appeal to the children. Incidental entertainment, creative art stations, interactive talent, and

3

a fun, upbeat band or DJ are perfect for this type of group. Another event element that is affected by a family guest list is the menu. You can't very well expect kids to enjoy spicy tuna sushi, veal, or even chicken *satay*. When doing your menu planning, have kid-friendly choices. Peanut butter and jelly sandwiches with the crusts cut off, macaroni and cheese, and spaghetti are all fun alternatives for kids. Also be sure to have plenty. Sometimes the adults like these menu items as well!

Shopping mall grand openings are geared toward families, so fun, colorful, interactive entertainment is appropriate, such as these human floats. *(Marty Allen, Apex, NC.)*

- *Mostly men or mostly women.* If your group is predominately male or female, the two event elements most directly affected are decor and entertainment. For a primarily male-dominated event, we most likely wouldn't invest a lot of money in our budget on decor. Generally, men don't appreciate elaborate floral centerpieces or lavish boutique linens. Women, on the other hand, most likely would notice those details, and we would spend more to meet those expectations.
- *Do your guests know each other?* When guests don't know each other, we like to provide entertainment that is interactive or lots of incidental entertainment. The right entertainment can be engaging and spark friendly conversation, making your event fun, with plenty to do.
- *Out-of-towners.* If your guests are mostly from out of town, you'll need to be cognizant of your location choice and of what type of giveaway you choose. When guests are mostly from out of town, you'll need to chose a location that is, first, easy to find, second, located where your guests can

Keeping in mind that Nike's target demographic for its new shoe line was young, active, and predominately male, it was cost-effective and appropriate to skip flowers and get clever with the new product—frozen shoes. *(Mel Hill Photography.)*

Jellyeye, a unique theatrical drum troupe, can peak your guests' curiosity, sparking conversation between guests who don't know each other. *(PWEE Staff.)*

get a taxi easily, and third, accommodates both these factors, such as a hotel. Out-of-town guests may or may not have rental cars, and they may or may not be familiar with the host city. Choosing a location where your guests can stay and attend the event is the best. Deciding what to choose for giveaways is crucial when your guests are from out of town. If your guests have to pack suitcases and fly across country, the last thing they'll want to do is pack a cumbersome giveaway bag.

- *Work associates.* The type of entertainment you choose will be affected in part if your guests are work associates at a work function. Silly entertainment where guests are encouraged to make fun of themselves can bomb. Work associates don't put themselves out there like that. Interactive entertainment, such as a game show, can be especially effective, though. Encourage your guests to interact with one another, and give individuals a chance to shine and not just be embarrassed.
- *Number of guests.* Depending on the size of your group, the timing of your event, the menu you choose, and most directly, the location all will be factors of the number of guests. The capacity of your location will be the determining factor of how many people you'll be able to host. If you already

Fund-raisers are a great forum to get creative. This hole-in-one competition, where participants attempted to hit golf balls onto a floating green at Baltimore's Inner Harbor, combined sport, celebrity (Samuel L. Jackson), and the chance of winning a new car. *(Marty Katz.)*

have a guest count, then that number will be the determining factor on choosing a location. When planning the menu for your event, which we discuss in detail in Chapter 5, there are certain things you can do with a small group that you can't do with a large group. For example, French service is not recommended for a large group. As you do the timing for your event, you'll need plenty of people-moving padding in your event timeline for a large group. As you can expect, moving 500 people from one room for cocktails to another room for dinner will take considerably more time than moving 50 people.

The demographics of your guests are very important to the event process. The tone, tempo, and design of your event will be decided on in part by who your guests are.

What

What is your event? Is it a social event? A fund-raiser? A corporate event? The type of event you are hosting will shape how you plan and design it. A corporate anniversary party will be much different from a celebrity gala. The logistics and requirements alone are on separate ends of the party spectrum.

The three main types of events are social, corporate, and fund-raiser events. The most commonly thrown social events are weddings, showers, birthday parties, and bar and bat mitzvahs. When planning social events, the three event elements directly affected by what type of event you're hosting are the location, the entertainment, and your printed materials. Social events have the most flexibility for location choices. Weddings can be held anywhere from a beach, to a church, to your backyard, to a museum, to a mansion. Locations for social events are dictated only by capacity and availability.

The entertainment at a social event also has a lot of possibilities. Because guests at a social event usually all know each other (check out the "Who" section earlier in this chapter), all sorts of entertainment are at your disposal. Dance bands, salsa dance instructors, face painters, and balloon artists all work at a social event but may not do so well at a corporate event.

The event element that can be the most difficult to handle for a social event is the printed materials. The invitations, "save the date" cards, place cards, escort cards, programs, and table numbers all have to accommodate a set of social rules that most people feel they need to observe. For example, if you're planning a wedding, the invitation must be worded in one way if the parents are paying for the wedding, a different way if the bride and groom are paying for the wedding, and yet another way if everybody's paying for the wedding. While the social rules for invitation language have eased up in recent years, wording on an invite, all the way through the program, can be a big task to take on. We do have some suggestions for invitation language at the end of this book in the Appendix B.

Corporate events, on the other hand, have their own set of unwritten rules that must be observed, and figuring out the best timing for these events is the most difficult part of the production process. Knowing that breaking point between fun and boring and appropriate yet original appears to hinge on how well you time out the entertainment and the length of speeches or how long you allow for dinner. The pace of a corporate event most definitely will make or break the event, making it a success or a bomb. In Chapter 2 we discuss the importance of event timelines and provide details about how to manage the flow of an event and create a successful event timeline.

One of the unwritten rules of corporate event planning is appropriate entertainment. For example, we have a client who, while fairly conservative, also likes to have original entertainment that the public relations world would say holds a lot of "talk value." This client is partial to entertainment that its clients will remember, perceive as high value, and then associate with our client. In essence, how we entertain and host the group will reflect directly on our client. We wanted to have a fabulous salsa band with Brazilian dancers in traditional Carnivale costumes at one of their events. However, once we saw the "traditional Carnivale costumes," we knew that the thong bottoms with feather bikini tops would be just over that corporate line of appropriateness.

Another entertainment area you need to be careful with is comedians. Sometimes comedy can be too blue or not politically correct, so we always need to be mindful of whom we hire for which corporate group.

Fund-raisers can be touchy events to plan. You don't want to be too extravagant, yet you do want the party to be great enough that your guests know that they're getting something for their contributions. Fund-raisers have to walk that fine line between being wonderful enough to get people to keep attending every year and not so extravagant that it looks as if you're spending all the money raised. Budget is probably the key factor to watch when planning a fund-raiser. Two other event elements that are affected when planning a fund-raiser are the decor and entertainment choices. These two elements make a party its own. The decor and entertainment at an event can define that event.

What type of event you are putting together will show most directly how to pace your event. While the timing of any event is important, it is most crucial at a corporate function, where the atmosphere isn't quite as casual as at a family event or picnic. The timing at a corporate event often dictates the mood, but it's the entertainment that influences the tone at a social event or fund-raiser. Keep in mind what type of event you are hosting so that you can best apply your efforts to the most effective elements.

Bill Cosby's wholesome humor made him a good match for a performance at a benefit for a faith-based health care provider with Chicago's Cardinal Francis George in attendance. *(Jerry Daliege.)*

When

When is your event? This pertains to time of year, to the day of the week, to the time of day, and to the length of the party. Your answers to when will affect everything from the color palate, to the invitations, to the menu, to the entertainment.

The time of year for an event will dictate the decor for your party as well as the menu. Everybody's heard of the no white before Memorial Day or after Labor Day rule. Well, decor also is seasonal. For example, it's not appropriate to use white linen hemstitch fabric on your tables in the fall, just as using a heavy burgundy velvet on your tables in summer would not feel right.

You'll want to choose decor that best goes with the season of your event. Planning your menu is also seasonal. Based solely on seasonal produce, there are just certain things that are only available at certain times of the year. Just as corn is the best in the fall, watermelon is best in the summer, and stone crab claws are only available until May. Plan your menu to feature what tastes best for that time of year. Lastly, location is also seasonal. For example, Florida is a hugely popular location for conventions, but not during hurricane season. When do you want to have your event? Will your guests need to fly in from around the country? If so, hosting an event in the Northeast during the heavy snow season may not be your best option.

The budget and location for your event can be affected directly by the day of the week on which your event is to occur. Location and budget go hand in hand. They depend on each other. One sure way to make or break your budget is with your location choice. And one way to help your budget is to choose an off day of the week to host your event. Just as going on vacation during the high season is more expensive than during the off-season, the same holds true for venues and days of the week. Sunday through Thursday are off days for most venues, and as such, you may find that venues such as hotels or museums offer better deals on rental fees or food and beverage minimums. These two points can have a positive result on your budget bottom line.

The time of day of your event will affect the types of guest services you offer, as well as if you'll need lighting. For example if your event is in the evening or right after work, you'll want to have a coat/bag check. People coming straight from work most likely will have briefcases (especially if they took a cab to the event), or if it's a chilly evening, they'll likely have coats or jackets.

Also, the time of day affects the placement of valet service. If your event is on a weekday during rush hour, you may want to place your valet drop-off and pickup in a location that is away from a busy street. It would be safer. Evening events (especially in the winter when it gets dark sooner) will need lighting. While we talk about specific kinds of lighting in Chapters 4 and 5, here at least you need to know that a nighttime event will need general area lighting as well as atmosphere lighting.

How long your event is will be most apparent on your budget's bottom line. With all the services you'll need for your party (entertainment, venue rental, valet service, coat check, catering, etc.), comes a rate for the length of service. For example, most local live bands perform for three to four hours. If your event is such that you need the band for five hours, then you'll need to pay extra for overtime. The same theory applies to your caterer, your venue rental, and any other services you may need at your party.

Certain types of events, such as a topping-off ceremony for a new building, require the event to be held in daylight hours for the sake of safety and media coverage. *(Courtesy of Northwestern Memorial Hospital.)*

Choices for your event range from seasonal decisions to budget decisions. The sooner you can settle on all the *when* variables for your party, the sooner you can begin to pick out decor such as linens and flowers—and the sooner you can get a firm bottom line for your budget.

Where

Where do you *want* to have your event, and where *can* you have your event? The goal is to find a location that answers both these questions. Locations are right for endless reasons—availability, capacity, services offered, logistics, proximity—we can go on and on.

A historical site can have as much impact as any other event element. Soldier Field in Chicago, while full of logistical challenges, proved perfect for this all out-of-town group of 3,000. *(Matthew Kaplan Photography.)*

Do you have any ideas about where you want your event? Event locations begin to break down into two choices at the start. They are either indoors or outdoors. From there, venues vary in type, and we discuss this in depth in Chapter 2. The location for your party will be one of the first things to decide on in your event production process.

Outdoor events are obviously seasonal. Outdoor picnics in the Midwest or the Northeast are only options from late spring to early fall. Weather is your primary concern when planning an outdoor event, but how does that affect your event decisions. Know that when dealing with Mother Nature, you may need to spend more. Outdoor events can require tenting (either to get in from out of the rain or to find respite from the heat), and tenting can require air conditioning or heating. Tenting also can require flooring and carpet or turf. And if you're using a tent, you may need lighting, which also then requires power, which may or may not be available at your site, and if not, you may need to provide generators. And if you need generators, you'll need at least two because lighting should never be plugged into the

What's better for a celebrity softball tournament than a professional baseball field? Making the location and event fit together even better was that the teams were made up of professionals in other fields of play—from the NBA to top recording artists. *(Courtesy of Michael Jordan Foundation.)*

same generator as sound (lighting causes a buzz in the speakers). The logistics for an outdoor event can be quite complicated, but the rewards for an unusual event under the stars are remarkable.

Indoor events are convenient—most of the time. While you don't need to deal with the weather for an indoor event, you will need to deal with the rules of your location. Any venue, from hotel ballrooms to museums and/or historical landmarks, has a set of policies that must be met. Hotel ballrooms usually have the least amount of rules, whereas a historical landmark probably has the most. Some of the common policies that venues have in place that will affect your event directly are things such as a food and beverage minimum, no hanging decor from the walls, capacity requirements, or open-flame rules. Each venue is different, and when choosing a location for your event, you should fully investigate what rules you'll have to follow (see Chapter 2).

Lighting can create a beautiful effect, particularly at an outdoor event. The open surroundings provide a blank canvas for creativity. *(PWEE Staff.)*

Indoor events are also convenient for the inventory and guest services they can provide to you in-house. For example, hotels maintain an inventory of tables, chairs, and linens. They also provide other services (for an extra cost) for your event, such as valet, coat check, bathroom attendants, and elevator attendants. Having these types of services at your disposal makes producing your event much easier. A lot of other types of venues also can provide some of the same things. Museums sometimes provide some of the same equipment for events as well. The types of venues that are available to you are almost endless, and we go into greater detail about venues in Chapter 2.

Why

Why are you having this event? What is the event's purpose? Is it a fund-raiser that will benefit from an extensive silent auction? Are you celebrating a corporate anniversary or a wedding? Knowing the purpose will guide you in all your future decisions regarding the party. Keeping in focus the goal of the event will aid you in

Knowing the purpose of your event can lead to obvious decisions. For example, the rededication ceremony of the Statue of Liberty called for an elaborate fireworks show choreographed to music. *(PWEE Staff.)*

budget decisions, decor decisions, and where you should host your event, along with countless other choices that you're going to make.

16

Charity Events

The first type of event to consider is the charity event. There are charity galas, luncheons, fashion shows, and races, and the list goes on. Raising money is always the purpose of a charity function. Yet the nuances between a charity gala and a charity race are caverns apart.

At a charity gala, the purpose is to give the attendee an event that in some way matches his contribution of the ticket price. As such, charity galas tend to be elaborate in decor, entertainment, and menu. Because the ticket price of a seat or table at a charity gala can be in the thousands of dollars, guests are treated to a memorable, elegant event. This can be translated into name talent, a four-course dinner, and lavish floral displays and linens.

At the other end of the charity spectrum is the charity race. Attendees are asked to contribute in the manner of an entrance fee or sponsor dollars for their run. Attendees expect very different things from a 10-kilometer run than from a gala dinner. At a charity race you'll need to provide the basics, such as a professional route, water stations, and fruit at the end of the race. Successful charity runs host a long list of sponsors who staff tents at the finish line, handing out donated products such as energy bars, water, bagels, and T-shirts. To set your race apart from others, you can have live music. Since the purpose of any charity event is to raise money, you'll also want to think about having a silent or live auction or both.

Social Events

Social events are weddings, birthdays, anniversaries, or cultural rites of passage such as a bar mitzvah or first communion celebration. Social events are unique to the decision process in that they are very personal and individual. Each event's purpose is distinctive and faceted to the person hosting it. What matters most to one person may not mean anything to the next, even though the two are planning the same type of event. For example, when planning a wedding, one bride may think that the ceremony is the most important part of her event, and as such, she devotes the bulk of her budget to paying for a high-end location, elaborate flowers, and an expensive dress. Another bride may think that the party is the most important part, spending most of her budget on the menu and a live band. In the first example, the bride felt that the purpose of her event was the meaning of the ceremony, the pomp and circumstance of the wedding tradition. In the second example, the bride felt that the celebration with family and friends was the purpose of her event.

Social events are the only ones where the purpose can swing very differently from person to person. Whatever the social event that is being planned, the purpose will be found within the person planning it or the person the party is for.

17

Corporate Events

Corporate events are the opposite of social events. Each one is quite specific in its purpose, and because of this, making choices can be infinitely easier for a corporate event than for a social event. At the same time, though, the common thread of corporate events is perception. As we've mentioned before, sometimes perception of what has been spent is more important than what actually was spent.

There are so many types of corporate events. The most common are meetings, product launches, anniversaries, holiday parties, and picnics. It seems that almost every company, small or large, hosts one or more of these kinds of events.

- *Meetings.* Even though there are all sorts of meetings (dealer meetings, sales meetings, departmental meetings, and conferences), the purpose for each one is the content. What are you meeting about? The conveyance of the content will be the most important part of your event. How are you presenting the content for your meeting? There are several ways to do this. You can have speakers, a video presentation, a panel of contributors, hand-outs, booths, and a question and answer session. The best way to present the content for your meeting will depend on your budget.
- *Product Launches.* A successful product launch is measured by the amount of exposure that the new item garners. Good exposure is generated with good timing and great creativity. If your product launch warrants media at-

Exposure is the most important element when launching a new product. The JumboTron, in Times Square, in the middle of the day is the essence of exposure. *(Jon Simon.)*

Trade shows are about foot traffic and exposure to your exhibit booth. Combining two seemingly unrelated ingredients, such as fashion and cars, can generate a buzz at a typical trade show, garnering crowds and exposure. *(www.jeffellisphoto.com.)*

tendance, you'll need to time the event so that the media is able to attend and then able to report on the event in a timely manner. For example, to make the afternoon news, a product launch would need to happen in the early morning. To make the evening news, the product launch would need to happen in the early afternoon. If you miss those attendance windows, you won't get the media to come. The next best way to get product exposure is a unique, creative launch.

- *Anniversaries.* The most important event element for a corporate anniversary is the guest list. Who are you inviting? Corporate anniversaries, particularly big ones (such as a fiftieth or seventy-fifth anniversary), always have a lot of people to thank, acknowledge, and therefore invite. If your company is national, you can't realistically invite everyone to fly in to attend the party. Therefore, do you have a party in every major market? Do you break it up into departments? Do you just invite the department heads? Putting together your guest list will let you know what kind of party you'll need to plan.

Smaller corporate anniversaries are a little easier to plan. Once again, the guest list will determine the event elements. For example, if everyone in the firm is invited, then you'll want to time the event for a slower time of year. While it's nice to try to time the party to the exact month or week of inception, you don't want to plan a party for a busy time of year. What determines the busy time of year is what kind of company the event is for. For example, if you're at an accounting firm, don't plan the party for the end of March, which is during the height of tax season.

- *Holiday Parties.* These types of corporate events are all about the food, entertainment, location, and timing. Holiday parties are just about having fun. Any good party is defined by the menu and the music. Make sure that you have good things to eat, which doesn't necessarily mean expensive. During the holidays especially, comfort food, which generally costs less than fancy food, most likely will go over best. Then there's the music. Festive equals good music. Choose entertainment, incidental, DJ, or live band, based on who's attending, but be sure that it's upbeat and fun.

    The success of a holiday party also hinges on the convenience of the location and the timing of the entertainment. Location convenience is based on how easy it is to get there and how safe it is to get home. Make sure that your site is easy to find and centrally located. More important, make sure that your guests can either stay at your location (such as a hotel) or that transportation is available. You don't want intoxicated guests driving home. Set an upbeat tone for your event with plenty of entertainment. We talk about the timing for an event in Chapter 2.

- *Picnics.* These events are similar to holiday parties because they are also defined by entertainment, location, and timing. While holiday parties usually are geared toward adults, company picnics usually are geared toward adults and children. Picnic entertainment is different from that for other types of events because you usually have a lot more activities (such as softball games, races, climbing walls, a bouncy house, etc.), along with music and incidental entertainment.

    The key for a successful company picnic is the location. An outdoor setting, such as a park or a beach, makes a great spot for picnics. Because of the location, and depending on what part of the country the event is located, the timing for the picnic is crucial. In most parts of the country, an outdoor picnic would need to be held sometime between late spring and early fall. We discuss this later in this book, but the best resource for choosing a dry, warm, sunny date for your outdoor company picnic is the *Farmer's Almanac.*

Maybe more than any other event essential, the *why* of your event will be your map to good decisions. Possessing a conscious, front-of-the-mind reason for why you're having an event can give clear direction on which road to take when you inevitably need to make difficult choices.

How

How much is in your budget? At this early stage, you may not know what things cost (we go over budgets in Chapter 3), but you should have an idea of what your maximum spend can be. Your bottom line will play a part in every decision you make for your event. From the location, to the menu, to number of guests, to the flowers, it's important to stay close to your budget. Notice how we said *close*. As with many things in life, event planning has its surprises. You may encounter a few unforeseen obstacles in the course of your event. If your budget is completely firm, you may want to set aside a small contingency percentage to cover any surprise challenges. In this way, you have a little room to work with.

21

With a contingency in the budget, additional guests and tight square footage challenges were met by spending a little extra and putting the stage over the pool. *(Courtesy of MDM Group.)*

If your budget is firm and you simply cannot exceed it, you'll need to refer to your five *W*s. Who are your guests? What is important to them? Knowing your guests can help you to make the choice between a more expensive band, for example, and a more expensive menu. Which would your group get the most out of?

What is your event? Is it a wedding, a corporate anniversary party, or a charity gala? Keeping in mind the type of event you're throwing will make decisions easier, such as choosing a giveaway for your guests. At something like a wedding, a small, homemade, thoughtful gift (such as chocolates or desserts) is appropriate and appreciated. Choosing a branded gift such as personalized golf tees, key chains, or T-shirts works better at a corporate event. And for charity events, a donated gift such as a crystal or silver calendar frame can be perfect for your guests.

When is your event? Choosing the time of week for your event can affect your budget significantly based on venue rental fees, food and beverage minimums, and even better rates for entertainment. The same goes for opting for a date that is during the off-season. For example, hotel room rates are considerably less for an off-season time than for a high-season time. Keep track of your event timeline, and you can cut back on overtime for bands, your caterer, and even your rental fees.

Where is your event? If your event is outside, vulnerable to the weather, you can expect the bottom line of your budget to be high. As we discussed earlier, outside events can require services that indoor events provide at no extra cost. Protection from the elements, electricity, a loading dock, and even a flat floor for your equipment are all things that are readily available in a venue such as a hotel ballroom.

Why is your event happening? When decisions become difficult, the best way to choose is to know why your event is happening. If your budget doesn't allow for everything you want, such as expensive linens, an abundance of flowers, the best live bands, and really high-end giveaways, you can remember why your event is happening and then make choices based on what works best for the cause of your event. For example, if you're putting together a new product launch for your company and you have to choose between expensive linens and a lavish giveaway bag for members of the media attending the event; you know that spending the money on the giveaway bag is the best way to maximize your return.

The answers to these questions are not just arbitrary choices that happen to come together in a cohesive fashion. These answers have now become your event priorities. Keep your goals in focus, and refer to them when making any decision—especially when you're up to your chin in details and you wake up in the middle of the night in a panic because you're not sure if the hydrangea hue in the centerpieces accurately picks up the coordinating color of the left gobo shining on the stage

Surprising event elements can punctuate your message—as this ballet performance at a ground-breaking for a women's hospital. *(John Reilly Photography.)*

backdrop. Just remember that your guests are there because you're celebrating your company or a new product or you're raising money to find a cure or that what's important is that the food is good and that your message, whatever it might be, is heard.

If you've answered the five *W* questions and the *how,* you're looking at the framework of your event. You've answered the critical questions. You've begun to visualize the party. You might even ask yourself, "Do I need professional help?" This pun was *totally* intended. If you *might* need help, you *absolutely* need help. If you think you can do it all by yourself, you may find that you are in over your head, and you might need "professional help." Let's face it, most people don't plan a dinner party without asking someone for help. Whether it's a caterer or a florist or someone to help with the decor, you will find that you'll enlist the help of several people through the course of planning your event. And we'll discuss all these people in the course of this book, as well as how to complete each step in the questions you answered in this chapter.

At the end of the day, we think that it's important to keep your perspective. Planning an event is full of decisions to make. But these are also fun problems to solve and fun decisions to make. Above all else, have fun with it!

Step Two: Take Care of the Nuts and Bolts

After you've finished the first step of prioritizing and envisioning your event, you've now thought through your event or what you hope it could be. Now you're probably wondering where to go from here. Your next move is actually a two-layer process that you can work on together—timing and location. Which is most important to you?

Because you may already have a location in mind, and because choosing a location causes a chain reaction affecting every detail of event planning, let's start with timing as our first operational step.

Timing Is (Almost Always) Everything

When is your event? This seems so straightforward, but ask 10 people this question, and you could get 10 different answers—the most common being, "I don't know." That's okay; let's first discuss what we're really asking. This is actually a trick question, and your answer may have many layers.

- What time of year? What season? Is it daylight savings time?
- What month are you considering? Is your month a high-season month?

- What day of the week is best? Must it be a Friday or a Saturday? Is it a long weekend?
- What time of day is your first choice? Sunset, sunrise, luncheon, or brunch?

Even if you know that you're throwing a Fourth of July party, you still need to determine when you start and how you should finish. Or maybe you know that you want a fall wedding, but what month is best for flowers, and should it be in the day or evening or on the weekend? We can't stress the importance of this question. Your answer can dictate location, entertainment, menu, decor, and most definitely budget.

Picking a Date

Our best advice is to let the timing come to you. A single factor will dictate what your date should be, and that's where you begin. What is that single factor? It's different for every person and every event. First, when choosing a date, there are really three timing issues to consider: time of year, time of week, and time of day. What is your event? Is it a fund-raiser? Meeting? Product launch? Holiday party? Grand opening? Company picnic? With the type of event in mind, what is your ideal setting?

Let's start broadly with time-of-year dates. Events that are this open-ended are usually conferences and meetings, company picnics, galas, holiday parties, and weddings. These types of events are timed to seasons or a particular month.

Conferences and Meetings

There are really only a couple of no-no dates for conferences or meetings. They are the big holidays (Christmas, New Year's, and Easter) and Super Bowl weekend. It's not a successful conference without attendees, so hosting a convention or conference that overlaps with any of these times will kill your attendance. Other than avoiding these times of the year, you'll want to know the season and the state in which you plan to have the conference. For example, Florida is a very popular destination for conferences, but Florida during hurricane season or the humidity of July or August is probably best avoided.

Company Picnics

These are some of our favorite events. They're down and dirty, with lots of comfort food and fun activities for the whole family. These are usually held in the summer, especially if you don't live in a mild climate. A picnic allows you to be flexible with your dates, in that a Saturday can work just as well as a Sunday. For your best options, consider a unique site. A lot of companies choose parks with playgrounds and built-in benches, but we particularly enjoy forest preserves, open grassy fields, and beaches because they lend us the best opportunity for creative license and a private space just for our clients. These locations can get snapped up quickly as

27

A wide-open outdoor space allows an eclectic company of actors, musicians, puppeteers, and mask makers to create a parade and stage a performance filled with theater, music, and dance that entertains families at an event. *(John Reilly Photography.)*

well, so you'll want to start investigating availability as soon as possible. We like to schedule company picnics when the kids are out of school and it's a slow time of year for the company, say, after the end of the fiscal year.

Galas

The season for galas is usually the fall. Everyone is in town, and there aren't many competing holidays. Because there is a season for galas, the best thing to do when choosing a date is to do your homework. A lot of organizations have similar guest lists, so you won't want to have your event on the same night as another gala and compete for the same attendance. Have your top three choices (going through the same process as for weddings), and begin to check venue availability. You'll quickly find out what's going on around town by who has holds on which space.

Holiday Parties

These actually can be the hardest dates to nail down, even though a St. Patrick's Day party is always on March 17! If you're throwing a Christmas/holiday party, you really have only two to three weekends to choose from, and everybody wants the coveted Saturday dates at every local hotel ballroom. Just don't discard Fridays,

This gala, held during the summer, was the finale of a two-week museum grand opening celebration. *(John Reilly Photography.)*

Holiday parties don't always have to be red linens and mistletoe, streamers, and balloons. For this New Year's event, the four walls of a normally bland space were transformed into a blues lounge. *(PWEE Staff.)*

and even Thursdays can make for a fun (and more cost-effective) party. Your best bet for getting a good date is to reserve your space early—some time in the summer. Or you can be really flexible and consider a Thursday date.

If your holiday party is one you're hosting at your home, you'll want to eliminate obvious travel weekends (such as the week just prior to Christmas and the week just after New Year's), and you may consider late November as an option because a lot of people have work party obligations as well.

Weddings

Start with the vision of your ceremony. Are you indoors at a church or temple? Or are you on a beach? An indoor wedding allows you to choose from four seasons, an outdoor wedding dictates a warmer month. If you can narrow down to a season, you can begin a process of elimination. Limit your choice to two months of the year, check those months for major holidays, and remove those weekends. Next, remove weekends that conflict directly with family obligations (such as vacations, business trips, etc.). What you have left are optimal weekends to take to a selection of venues where you can check availability.

29 ▶

With the right lighting, decor, and space, even a room at a member's club can feel "spiritual." *(John Reilly Photography.)*

If you're having trouble narrowing a date down to two months, find your key factor. Do you have a favorite flower that must be in the bouquet? Find out when that flower is in season, choose from those months when it's readily available, and you'll even save on your floral design budget. Do you have your heart set on a location? Call the venue to check availability, and let the venue narrow your choices for you. Is the bride wearing her mother's gown and it has a full-length wool coat to go over it? Attire (especially the bride's) can be a clear indicator of what time of year to choose.

Choosing the time of week to have your event can have the most impact on your budget. We cover in detail in Chapter 3 why the next statement can alter your bottom line significantly. Knowing that Saturdays are *the* most popular day of the week for events, are you flexible enough to pick another day? Food and beverage minimums, talent availability and cost, transportation availability, negotiation power, and virtually everything else is at a premium on a Saturday. Be open to Thursdays, Fridays, and Sundays for your event.

When tackling the issue of timing for multiday events such as corporate conferences, your optimal timing is for the conference or meetings to take place at the beginning of the week. Your guests' attention span is much longer and sharper on a Tuesday than on a Friday afternoon.

Unlike the time-of-week decision, where factors are based on guests, time-of-day decisions are also based on event elements. For example, if you have an event with a fireworks finale, you'll need to set your start time for early evening if you consider daylight savings time. If your event includes a show with lighting, again, you'll need the cover of darkness for your show to be effective. Press events, such as grand openings, or press announcements need to be earlier in the day so that media representatives can make their evening news deadlines. Lastly, a religious event, such as a first communion, bar mitzvah, or wedding, also has timing traditions. These and countless other factors will have an impact not just on the start time but also on the end time of an event. Prioritize the elements of your event in order to determine the best time of day to enjoy it.

Tips for Picking the Right Date

- If your event is outdoors, consult the *Farmer's Almanac.* It may seem strange, but this book is right more often than the meteorologists. If you can't decide between dates, look them up in the *Farmer's Almanac,* and go with whichever one has the least chance of rain. For one wedding we planned, the *Almanac* had the same chance for rain on consecutive Saturdays. Since there wasn't a preference between the two available dates, we chose the one that had the full moon for added romance. Everyone kept asking if we planned it and then thought we were joking when we replied, "Yes!"
- Compare your date with your town's/city's calendar. If you had a choice, you wouldn't want guests coming to town when there's a huge convention or the busiest tourist weekend of the year. Hotel rooms and flights cost significantly more during those times. Also, we've run into permitting problems in smaller towns when there were two large events happening on the

same night. In smaller towns, parking, transportation, and city services such as traffic control can be stretched too thin for two large events.

- If budget is a concern, go for the out-of-season time rather than high season (which seems to apply to most places except southern California). You'll have more negotiating power and a cost-effective budget if you plan your event out of high season.
- Check for holidays that surround your event. If your event is on a holiday weekend, you'll want to provide out-of-town guests with plenty of suggested activities. In some cases you may want to choose a different date in order to gain a higher attendance.
- Your chosen date will affect your event start time. A Thursday night party will start earlier than a Saturday night party, and Sunday events are usually during the day. If your date is during daylight savings, you also may want to consider a later start time depending on the type of event.
- The time of day for your event will affect your decor and your guests' attire. An evening event probably will require more lighting than an afternoon event. Also, evening events usually are more formal than daytime events.
- Depending on what is happening on your event day (holiday, rush hour, festivals, Super Bowl, etc.), consider how that should (if at all) affect your event. Do a little research so that you can anticipate your guests' experience and what they might want and need.

The Flow of an Event

Once you have an idea of when your event will be, you next need to consider how your event timing will set the tone of your event. Through our experience planning major events, we know that a well-timed event never feels rushed but also isn't boring. We also know that the best events have an ambiance of a buildup, beginning with interesting elements and consistently rising to an exciting crescendo. With this in mind, we don't leave our guests exhausted; rather, we leave them wanting more, discussing for weeks afterwards about how much fun they had. Experience has taught us to walk this tightrope effectively, and so while each event is different (even annual ones that happen year after year), there is a process to creating a good "flow" for your event.

At this stage of your project, you'll want to get a very rough idea for your event timeline. This timeline will change significantly as you progress through production, and we will help you to move from the preliminary event timeline to a final event timeline in Chapter 5. This preliminary event timeline will be an important tool as you contract and schedule vendors (Chapter 3), negotiate with your venue

Grand opening events need grand beginnings. The ribbon cutting ceremony, balloon release, and a local, university marching band set the tone for this new retail property's first day open to the public. *(Marty Allen, Apex, NC.)*

(see below), and coordinate general logistics (Chapter 6). Right now you need to get an idea of your start and end times.

What are you doing at your event? Are you serving dinner? Just dessert? Just cocktails and hors d'oeuvres? Do you have speeches, a band, a video, or a presentation? List your main activities for the event. Later we'll discuss how long typical activities take at events.

Now you're prepared to choose a preliminary start time. (That's right, stay flexible with your start time because you may need to bump it up or back depending on what comes up in your production process.) A general rule of thumb is that evening events during the workweek (Monday through Thursday) begin directly after business hours, about 6:00 to 6:30 P.M. The attire is usually business or cocktail but never formal because no one likely will have time to change after work and before your party. Since this is right after work, you'll want to feed your guests immediately. If it's a reception, make sure that you have an abundance of passed hors d'oeuvres and/or food stations.

In addition, you'll want to end the event early so that your guests can still get a bite to eat at a decent hour, usually by 8:00 or 9:00 P.M. If you're serving dinner, you'll still want to have plenty of food right away, but consider shortening your reception hour to get your guests in to dinner and sitting sooner. We generally like to have our workweek events that include dinner end by 10:00 or 11:00 P.M.

Friday events usually start before Saturday events but later than workweek events. People usually don't mind leaving work early on a Friday to change clothes for an event, so you could have a formal event on a Friday. Start times for Fridays can be anytime between 6:00 and 7:30 P.M. Friday events can go quite late as well. You definitely have more timing options with a Friday or Saturday event.

Saturday events can happen all day. You have much more flexibility because you don't really need to concern yourself with work schedules, traffic, school, and so on. A good start time for a day event is between 10:00 and 11:00 A.M. If you do start at 11:00 A.M., expect to serve your guests lunch. If you start after 2:00 P.M. and end by 5:00 P.M., you don't need to serve a meal, but you will need plenty of munchies. Saturday events, no matter what you're doing, generally are longer and more social. Guests like to linger, kibbutz, and go off their diets on Saturdays, so keep that in mind. Saturday evening events can end anywhere between 11:30 P.M. and the wee hours of the morning.

Sunday events usually are held during the day and early evening (unless it's a holiday weekend; then you'll work your timeline like it's a Saturday). We don't usually like to start Sunday events before 11:00 A.M. Sunday evening events can start as early at 5:30 P.M. and usually end by 10:00 P.M.

If you can pick your start time (remember it's preliminary) and estimate your end time, you're ready to fill in with the "meat" of your event. Here are some general guidelines for how long things take at parties. As you contract your vendors (in Chapter 3), they will help you to refine this schedule.

Receptions/Cocktail Hours

Just because it's called a cocktail hour does not mean that it should last 60 minutes. If this is a Saturday night event, 45 minutes for cocktailing can be plenty. If this is right after work on a Thursday, you may need 90 minutes to accommodate late arrivals from work. Also, allow lots of time for your guests to fill up a bit on food before they start with drinks (Remember, they haven't eaten since noon!). Of course, your reception hour also can just be 60 minutes.

Dinner Service

There's French service (where each guest is offered a selection from a silver platter, usually the entrée, and then from a number of side dishes); there's English service (where each course is served on the plate and waitstaff offers dressing for salads, breads, or even ladled soups); and then there's plated service, where the first course is set before your guests are seated. As you can surmise, French service takes the longest, and plated service is a good time saver. French service is usually only appropriate for a smaller guest count, and some venues won't even offer it. French service can consume up to 15 minutes per table of 10 to 12 people depending on your venue's (or caterer's) proficiency. English service is what most of us are accustomed to, and all venues offer this. If your venue is particularly efficient (ask if you don't know), English service is quick, about 5 minutes per table of 10 to 12 people. If you need the pace of your event to be time-economical, consider presetting your first course. Presetting your first course can trim your service by10 to 15 minutes.

Dinner service can become very elegant simply by adding an intermezzo of sorbet. *(Richard Shay Photography.)*

Breakfast, Lunch, and Dinner

Breakfasts and brunches can take an hour or more. Lunches are quick; allot 30 to 45 minutes. Dinners (once served) usually take 45 minutes.

Coffee Service

If you include your coffee cup and saucer in your place setting, all the waitstaff must do is arrive with pots of decaffeinated and regular coffee and place the cream and sugar on the table. This takes no time at all (about five minutes per table) and is not too loud, so it can be served while you show a video or engage in another activity you have planned. Another option is to offer each guest a cup and saucer and then serve the coffee. This takes quite a bit longer, usually requires more staff, and can happen during dessert service. Allot about 10 minutes for this process.

Shows

Do you have a band that's putting on a show? Or maybe a comedian? We prefer shows to last no longer than 45 minutes. Remember, leave them wanting more!

Culminating an event with a "wow" leaves a lasting impression. For this film premier finale of *Brother Bear,* guests were surprised with a three-song performance by Phil Collins, whose music was featured on the movie's soundtrack. *(PWEE Staff.)*

Speeches and Videos

These are always important but not generally the most fun parts of an evening. Videos shouldn't be longer than three to six minutes (three is usually best). Speeches are best when they're short (one to three minutes), but they usually end up being five minutes. When it comes to hired speakers (or keynote speeches), the timing is a little different. Your overall program sets the pace. For example, if you're planning a conference and you've hired a speaker to kick off or close the

Some speakers are interesting before they even open their mouths. When two supercelebrities, such as Oprah Winfrey and Denzel Washington, are your hosts, it's not necessary to fret about speech length. *(Courtesy of Michael Jordan Foundation.)*

conference, her speech will be longer (probably around 10 minutes). If you have a featured speech that includes a video presentation, that will be even longer. The only rule set in stone is that shorter is better than longer.

Ceremonies

It seems like all ceremonies, ribbon cuttings, weddings, and award presentations should never be longer than an hour. It's usually better if they're shorter, but ceremonies usually have their own protocol and tradition, so you must accommodate.

People Moving

When we work with the same group annually, we get to know their crowd. For example, we know that with one of our groups, even though there are 1,200 of them, we can get them seated in a ballroom for dinner in 15 minutes. They're movers! It is not customary for this large number to move so quickly, but they do, every time. The four factors to work with when inserting people-moving times are

When it comes to a ribbon cutting or dedication ceremony, the most important factor is the media shot. You'll want to make sure that your staff photographer and any attending media are ready to capture the moment. *(John Reilly Photography.)*

- How many guests do you have? Larger numbers mean a longer time.
- Do your guests know each other? If they do, it's harder to get them to separate and move.
- Do you have help moving guests? If you have people to politely ask guests to join them in the next room, it can speed it along.
- How far are you going? Going from a ballroom foyer to the ballroom is relatively simple. If you're changing floors, that's more time consuming. Start with a 15-minute window and then add or subtract time based on these four factors.

For a 25-hour summer solstice event as part of a museum grand opening, arrivals took place literally around the clock. To alleviate crowds (and temper frustration), entrance-time tickets were distributed. *(John Reilly Photography.)*

Arrivals

This is another occasion where knowing your group can help you immensely. Some groups take 30 minutes for everyone to arrive; other groups (not our favorite) arrive 10 minutes early. If you don't know your group, assume that it will be early.

Dancing

We like to have dancing begin during dessert and go until the party's over.

Pad Your Elements

Give yourself plenty of time for the inevitable errors. Don't time things so closely that you have no room for error. Add five minutes to your people moving or be ready before your official start time so that you can breathe a little easier. Once you go over your timing with your vendors, they'll advise you as well.

Experience the Event

As you time the event, imagine the flow of the evening as if you were a guest. You'll know if it feels rushed, too slow, or just right. Bear in mind that once you get on site, your schedule probably will change, so stay flexible!

Site, Setting, Scene

A special event can be held almost anywhere. From the complicated (the Counting Crows on our client's private beach) to the more common (a wedding at a resort), each event has its own personality. While the host (be it your company, a city, a charity, or you) will establish your event's purpose, nothing will dictate atmosphere for your event's character like the location. In many cases the location choice will be your first decision. Do not underestimate the importance of accomplishing this task early on. When looking for your right location, bear in mind that what you want to communicate with your event also should be stated by your venue. In other words, what does your location say about your event?

A room's decor, as in a country club or a four-star hotel, can convey exclusivity, elegance, or style. The opposite is quite true as well. In themed restaurants, the atmosphere is silly and fun. Some other locations, such as museums or historical sites, can range from very hip and contemporary to unusual and luxurious. While a lot of people think that outdoor events lend to a more casual tone, with the right setting, an outdoor event can be quite formal as well. Look at the surroundings. The carpet, the walls, the lobby, the entrance, the neighborhood, the bathrooms,

The symphony conveys upscale elegance. Naturally, therefore, the symphony center stage for a dinner party will say the same. *(Richard Shay Photography.)*

and the services provided all will be part of the tone of your event and convey a message to your guests.

Location Cost Considerations

41

Your location choice will have a direct and significant effect on your bottom-line budget. From the up-front charges, such as a venue fee, to unseen logistics costs, such as providing your own power, the venue will dictate every single line item in your budget. The choices for venues are endless. Each choice and each challenge is unique to that site. Coming up we'll discuss the most used types of venues and the benefits and drawbacks of each one.

All-In versus a Blank Slate

Construction jobs have contractors that oversee every element of a build. They hire, manage, negotiate, and supervise everyone from the electricians to the

EVENT SUCCESS STORY: HOW TO WEATHER ANY STORM

When producing a corporate anniversary event for an asset risk management company, we encountered challenging weather-related obstacles. The client chose name talent and was set on the idea of having the event on the private beach next to the company's lake house. For our first challenge, we needed to flatten the sand with a beach excavator in order to accommodate the staging requirements for the band. The band called for a 40-foot-wide stage, so in addition to leveling the beach, we also hoped to widen the shoreline enough to allow for some room on the sides of the stage for catering to get through. (The only spot to locate the kitchen was backstage.) The week before the event, we did a site survey with the band's production manager, to view the newly flattened beach to see the layout and meet with the staging, sound, and lighting contacts and resolve some outstanding logistical issues. After much deliberation, the final locations of the stage, front-of-house platform, and lighting tower were placed. For the next two days, we appended and finalized our very tight load in schedule, and when Wednesday morning came around, we were ready to begin our three and a half day load in and setup. Despite the challenge of transporting the equipment through the sand (which will always slow down the load-in process) there was another hurdle to clear when the "all terrain" forklift couldn't navigate through the loosely packed sand, we found ourselves ahead of schedule at the end of the day Thursday evening.

First thing Friday morning we were met with yet another obstacle; we found that an overnight storm had created 10- to 12-foot waves (on Lake Michigan!), which had carved the shoreline

The tide begins to make its way upstage. *(John Reilly Photography.)*

inland by almost 25 feet. The first six stage-right platforms were wading in various levels of water, and there was so much sand erosion that the corners of the front-of-house platform hung just 6 inches above the ground. The client had chosen to forego weather insurance, which meant that there was no rain plan. At this point we had approached a fork in the road. One option was to leave the stage where it was and restructure the ground beneath the stage legs. While this option certainly was quicker, we ran the risk of either the production manager arriving on site, declaring the stage unsafe for his band, and canceling the performance or the weather flaring up again, causing more waves and recreating the same problem, possibly too close to event time for anyone to be able to fix.

Another option was to move the whole stage further inland. This posed an obvious threat to the timing of the setup and added sizable cost. To move the stage required the lighting truss to be taken down and all the lights removed; the entire stage to be dismantled, moved, and then reassembled; the lighting to be rehung on the truss, raised, and refocused; and then the sound equipment to be hung and tested. This would require the crew to work through the night, which would add considerable overtime to the labor and also would require additional work lights to be brought in, incurring yet another cost. After very thorough weather tracking and consultation with the client, we determined that the storm had passed completely and that it was worth the risk to stabilize the right edge of the stage. Ultimately, the band's production manager arrived and was satisfied with the stability of the stage, the weather held up, and the show went perfectly. The lesson to take from this is to never give up. Logistical obstacles and challenges almost always can be overcome.

Tenting on the beach. *(John Reilly Photography.)*

For this dealer meeting, the space needed to accommodate 2,000 guests, a 14-piece live band, food stations, 20-foot sculptures, and all the featured new vehicles. *(www.jeffellisphoto.com.)*

framers to the painters. Something for you to contemplate is this: Do you want to *be* the contractor, or would you like your venue to come equipped with one?

A good rule of thumb is that the more a site needs, the more expensive it will be at the end of the day. And the opposite is true. A beautiful restaurant with a private room may have a large up-front rental fee, but that location already has a kitchen, tableware, tables, chairs, decor, and maybe an existing valet service. Thus, adding it up, that up-front rental fee may be well worth it. Also, a lot of restaurants charge the fee but put it toward a food and beverage minimum. However, you'll have to work with their availability.

On the other hand, your backyard seems like it's free—but what do you need to provide? Depending on how many people are coming, you could need everything from forks to a tent with a floor, from a caterer to a generator for additional power. In addition, you'll need to coordinate all those vendors. However, your home can be so personal and intimate and a wonderful setting for an event.

So how ambitious do you feel? We don't believe that anything's impossible; we

44

This client's home made for a wonderful venue, particularly because it included a private beach. *(John Reilly Photography.)*

just know that we may need to adjust. Staying organized and focused is an essential tool for your successful event. For now, here are some costs associated with the more common and a few uncommon venues.

Hotels
Hotels usually have all of the basics that you'll need, but there are labor charges for bartenders, waitstaff, bellmen, and if you have technical requirements, electricians. Hotels generally are the most cost-effective venues but are commonplace.

Restaurants
You generally find a restaurant that fits your style, but you'll pay extra for a Friday or Saturday night. Some restaurants won't even consider a private party for a weekend night. They will have a lot of what you'll need to put on an event, even bathroom attendants. The hard part about restaurants is the logistics and constrictions. Restaurants usually don't have loading docks or easy delivery spaces for large or odd-sized boxes. They have limited storage for your deliveries (give-

One benefit of holding an event at a restaurant is using the existing design and decor. *(John Reilly Photography.)*

aways, linens, flowers, etc.), and as such, you'll need to be in and out of there in a day.

Convention Centers

If you have a lot of time and a lot of budget, convention centers can make great venues. They have *lots* of storage, easy delivery routes, big loading docks, huge spaces with high ceilings, and the capacity for as much as your creativity (and wallet) can muster. They are expensive. The majority of them are union houses, which require union labor, and that means a higher labor bill. You must hire union labor for everything—a union electrician to plug in anything, a union decorator to drop your linens, and a union supervisor for all of them. It can add up quickly!

Lofts/Warehouses/Empty Spaces

We've done cocktail parties and launch parties in warehouses and lofts, and let's just say that these are some of the most fun parties. Don't try to do anything formal because these spaces are raw, and that's what we love about them. They require a lot of imagination, but they can end up spectacular. Some spaces have amenities,

Opposite of a space with existing decor, a warehouse space leaves all options open for creativity and originality. *(Peter Wagner.)*

such as bathrooms, but don't count on it. You'll need to bring it all in, a temporary kitchen, portable bathrooms, valet service, lighting, power—you name it. These spaces are cheap, and those are the reasons why.

Tents

This is another fabulous blank palate in which to go wild with creativity. Depending on where your tent is erected, you may or may not need to provide amenities. They are expensive, but sometimes they are your only option. You can count on a few costs. Labor is the first, temperature control is second (heat or air conditioning or at least fans), and power to run your temperature, sound, lighting (check out Chapter 4), and kitchen will be needed (think coffee makers). After you have your basics, you need to decorate your event. It's costly and involved but not impossible.

Historical Venues

These are incredible statement makers. And they can be incredible pains in the butt! Historical venues have pages and pages of rules, preferred vendor lists, and outdated spaces. They also have loads of charm and usually don't need any help in the decor department. Expect to deal with a long list of logistics, be very flexible

The one thing with tents is that the decor must stretch much higher than the average hotel ball-room. In this tent, all 30 feet of height was used to splash around color, shapes, movement, and fabric. *(Matthew Kaplan Photography.)*

in what you want, and be close to your point of contact (see the next section). Historical venues are a little more expensive to rent, but they can make up for it in the bottom line because they don't require a lot of dressing.

Museums

Like historical venues, museums have lots of rules and most often a list of preferred vendors from which you must choose. Also like historical venues, museums don't need a lot of decor. Where you can get caught on bottom-line budget is with the amenities and setup times. You'll pay extra for valet, for going off the preferred vendor list, for docents, for storage, and for power if you have overtime. Get the punch list of extras before you sign on the bottom line, and make an informed choice.

Beaches and Parks

Nothing compares with the light at the beach. There is just something about the way the sun shines that makes the beach special. Parks have that same effect on people. Maybe parks make us feel young again. It makes sense that people love to have events at these locations, but there are a few things to consider. Permitting is one of them. Pulling permits isn't always expensive, but it's always time-consuming. And, because navigating through a city permitting department takes experience and patience, it is a cost consideration. Also, you have your guests to think about. How are elderly or disabled people going to traverse sand or grass? Is there nearby parking? It can be done (have custom platforms built for walkways), but what costs

Taking over three miles of South Florida's beachfront requires not only the harmonization of vendors but also the coordination of several city departments as well. *(Courtesy of MDM Group.)*

EVENT SUCCESS STORY:
DON'T LET SETBACKS STOP YOU FROM THINKING BIG

A computer software client challenged us with creating a one-of-a-kind event that would blow away their 3,000 VIPs who were in town for a conference. We came up with the idea of taking over Chicago's venerable Soldier Field to erect a tent that spanned from end zone to end zone and included several name entertainment performances, and closed with fireworks shot from the north stands. We negotiated and contracted the venue; obtained all the licenses, permits, and insurance necessary to hold an event of this type; and we were on our way. We worked closely with the venue and brought in a grass expert to ensure the integrity of the field, to determine how we could set up a tent of this size and what type of flooring we should use inside the tent. We then created a security and crowd control plan and determined the ingress/egress for the guests. After determining where the guests would be arriving at the site, we hired and coordinated shuttles for all 3,000 guests to arrive from various hotels as well as the convention center. We also negotiated and contracted all the talent, and began to coordinate all the travel, production, and hospitality details required for each one. Everything seemed to be moving along beautifully. We had put together our load-in schedule, sent it off to all of the vendors, and then arranged for our big production meeting at the site.

Keeping in mind that our event start time was 6:00 P.M. Monday evening, we were informed at the production meeting (one week before the event), that the midday Sunday Chicago Bears game had been moved from noon to a 3:00 P.M. kickoff. And, as a result of the later

The clear-top custom tent stretches Soldier Field from end zone to end zone. *(Matthew Kaplan Photography.)*

start-time, we would not take possession of the field until 7:00 P.M. that night, for an event set to begin at 6:00 P.M. the following day! Just to make it more interesting, we also were told that the tent could not be secured in the normal fashion of staking it into the ground because blueprints of the underground watering system did not exist. And so the crisis management began. How do you erect over a 100-yard tent without staking, with three hours less time? And, if it was possible, could a solution be concocted in a week's time?

Our first call was to the tent company to develop a plan B to avoid staking into the ground, which included 5,000-pound concrete blocks at each one of the staking points (every 20 feet) all the way around the tent. Then we had to come up with a plan to deliver and set the concrete blocks in place and have them picked up after the event. And, what sort of machinery lifts 5,000-pound concrete blocks, moves them around, and places them? Normally, a load-in and setup for an event of this size would consume a couple of days, but we had 23 hours. We ordered a special crane to bring the blocks in that got stuck in the player's tunnel and had to have the air let out of its tires to make it through. We got this problem solved around midnight, and we were sure that we were doomed. Somehow, however, the tent company worked through the night and got everything in place while the staging, sound, and lighting company waited impatiently to begin its load-in and setup to ensure that it was ready on time for the numerous rehearsals and sound checks that all had to take place before the guests arrived at 6:00 P.M. The swirling October wind coming off nearby Lake Michigan compounded the already challenging situation. We brought in extra personnel to get everything done on time, and as always, our incredible team of staff and vendors managed to make a miracle happen yet again.

The guests arrived taking in all the history of Soldier Field and realizing that they were standing on the field where some of the greatest teams in football had played, never knowing that

there had been any issues at all. The concert went off without a hitch as the guests danced on the tables. The food was delicious, and the fireworks were perfectly choreographed to music. But this one will go down in the books as one of the most difficult ever.

Even with one hurdle after another, we knew that the most important element of our client's night was to host this event at Soldier Field. Working in a historical venue and working around a schedule like a kickoff time for a nationally televised NFL game can produce a long list of challenges. Since the most important aspect of this event was location, simply moving to another venue to avoid these difficult challenges was not an option. Remember to have your event prioritized, and you'll know then which challenges are worth fighting through and which are worth avoiding completely.

Fireworks light up the night sky. *(Matthew Kaplan Photography.)*

51

are you willing to pay for? In addition, beaches and parks aren't equipped with 120-amp circuits, so again, you'll need power. It's not impossible (we had a party for 350 on a private beach featuring the Counting Crows), but you need to weigh your options.

Point of Contact

While mulling over your location choices, you likely will be assigned a point person for the venue. This is the person who will put a hold on the date(s) for you; coordinate site surveys, tastings, and walk-throughs with vendors; and generally give you advice. When you do finalize your venue choice, your point person (banquet captain, special events coordinator, banquet manager, catering director, sales manager, rental events manager, conference services manager, or catering/conference planner—the list could go on, but you get the idea) is the first person you call when you have a problem or a question, the first person you find when you're on site and need anything, and the first person you thank when your event is perfect. Working with your point person can be a delicate relationship that is kept in balance or thrown off balance by personalities, day-to-day situations, and attitude.

The best advice we can give you about working productively with your point person is threefold:

1. *Make contact right away. Get them invested in your project. Keep them involved.* You need them. Make sure that they know that you know that you need them. If you have a working relationship with your point of contact person from the very beginning, that person becomes committed to your event, almost as much as you. And that's what is needed for a successful event. *Everyone* needs to care about the project. The first step is to involve your contact person as soon as possible and often after that.

2. *Respect the person's position of authority and experience in the space.* Get the person on your side. If or, rather, when you need to break the rules, you will need the support of your contact person. When you need something special or something the venue doesn't normally do, you will need the support of your contact person. When you are settling your final bill, you will need the support of your contact person. Your contact person knows the space better than anybody (unless he's a rookie). The person's experience will be helpful to you, and you should take advantage of it. Your point of contact also knows every person who works in the venue and will be instrumental on event day when things need to get done.

3. *Don't go around or above your contact person (unless absolutely necessary).* Just as in any professional situation, there are channels to run through and red tape to wade through. Having said these two things, sometimes you get sticklers for the rules or a nonbeliever. Your event is unique to you, and as such, you may have ideas for your event that are also unique to the site. For example, if you want to suspend food stations from the ceiling and you know it's possible but your banquet captain is against it, you must first try to make your point person a believer. You'll have an easier time if you and your point person want the same things. On the other hand, if you've tried everything you can to sway your point person to accepting your fabulous ideas, then you may need to go around that person. Part of successful event planning is not taking no for an answer, finding an alternate solution, or finding someone else (vendor, venue, or contact person) who believes in the impossible just like you. Along with that, a successful event producer knows when she's hit the wall and it's time to adjust.

Whoever ends up being your main point of contact, if at all possible, make friends with that person. You will be working with that person on a day-to-day basis, and on event day, the two of you will be spending long hours together. Remember that your point person wants a successful event just like you do. If you follow these three rules, you'll have a better chance of pulling it off with his help.

Questions to Ask

- Get any information you can regarding access to your space—not just access for your guests, but also dock space, delivery areas, freight elevators, dedicated elevators, and storage. If you have limited access or access that is not dedicated for load-in and tear-down, expect your labor costs to be a little higher. If guest access to the space is difficult (such as a dirt pathway or lots of stairs), provide alternate routes for elderly guests or guests wearing high heels.
- Find out when you have access to the space for setup and when you must be cleared out from tear-down. Also, some spaces only allot a certain number of hours for the event itself. If you have a preliminary timeline together, you'll know whether your timing is right or not. There may be charges if you need to load-in early or if your load-out takes overtime.
- Ask what other events are happening at the same time as yours at your venue. Make sure that you are comfortable that your venue will be able to

handle more than one event at a time. Multiple events will strain valet, the kitchen, courtesy golf carts, and so on.

- Get that list of preferred vendors or exclusive vendors! There can be extra charges if you don't use their vendors, so include that in your budget. Ask if you can go off their list. Ask for credentials on all vendors, and find out how long they've been working in that space.
- If your event is outside, find out about local noise ordinances. This may affect your event timeline.
- Ask to see the bathrooms your guests will be using. If they're not clean, you have every right to request that they be cleaned immediately before your event.
- When estimating capacity, ask to see photos or floor plans that match your capacity so that you can judge the space for yourself. You may want a roomier feel.
- Ask if your contact person will be at your event. You want the person that will be working with you for the next few weeks or months to be on site.

Tips for Site-Selection Success

- Have a few (or at least two) dates to choose from.
- Do your homework on estimated costs (see the questions section) so that you can minimize surprises, do a cost comparison, and then make an informed decision.
- If your event is outdoors, subject to the weather, check the *Farmer's Almanac* for your best date. It is still the most reliable weather forecast resource available.
- Try to anticipate your guests' needs, such as wheelchair access, limited parking, nearby bathrooms, temperature, and so on.
- Plan around existing events—holidays, long weekends, festivals, summer vacations, and so on.
- Be flexible!

3

Step Three:
Create a Project Blueprint

At this point, do you have a worn-out folder full of papers, pictures torn out of magazines, and maybe two or three venue brochures? It's kind of spilling all over, and you're not quite sure what to do with it? Maybe you've sat down and looked over it all and wondered what to do with all the information and what it all means. Most important, you're not sure how you exactly go about putting this event all together. How do you start producing the event?

Since you've hopefully chosen a date and a venue at this point (or at least narrowed your list to two or three), you are ready to begin a blueprint of your event. The project timeline and the budget are the blueprint that you and your vendors will follow in putting this event together. You'll first organize your work done so far and then create a way to maintain that organization. Then you'll break down your budget, giving yourself boundaries for how, when, and what to spend your money on.

Be Organized

Build an Event Book

The first step in being organized is to gather all the information you've collected so far, as well as any notes you may have on locations, any magazine cutouts where

As part of this grand opening celebration's production process, a stage treatment needed to be designed and approved before construction actually could begin. *(Rendering by Production Plus.)*

you might have gotten some ideas, or any business cards you may have collected from potential vendors, your event, and then begin the process of organizing your *event book*. All you need for an event book is an empty binder, page separators with tabs, a three-hole punch, and a pen. As you go through your notes and papers, organize them into sections that make sense to you. Some of the most common sections we use are listed below. You can use all these or create your own combination.

> Contact Sheet (See Appendix A)
> Contracts
> Correspondence To
> Correspondence From
> Budgets
> Operations (Check out Chapter 6)
> Food and Beverage
> Decor
> Insurance
> Venue
> Floor Plans
> Guest Lists
> Sound and Lighting
> Timelines

Seating Plans
Expenses
Transportation
Notes
Miscellaneous

We don't always use every one of these sections for every event, and because each event is different, we frequently add in a unique tab specific to that party. For example, when we produced the grand opening of the Aladdin Hotel in Las Vegas, we needed a tab section labeled "Camels and Horses." This is not exactly something you would use every time. Sometimes events that seem similar won't have the same organization. For the grand opening events of the Borgata Casino in Atlantic City, we didn't need "Camels and Horses," but we did need a section labeled "Casino Control Commission." On the other hand, there are common denominators for *every* event book. They are the "Contact Sheet," the "Correspondence" sections, the "Contracts" section, and the "Miscellaneous" section.

We print *every* significant correspondence with our clients, vendors, or venue. That includes letter and e-mails. In this way, all important decisions are in writing and in the book for easy reference and backup. You'll want the same easy reference for your contracts as well. Contracts include lots of important information, such as arrival times, compensation, contact information, and so on. The "Miscellaneous" section is the catchall. It's great for all those papers that don't have a specific home in your book.

Here are some sample event book sections that we've used in the past:

Destination Wedding	Company Picnic	Charity Gala
Contact Sheet	Contact Sheet	Contact Sheet
Contracts	Contracts	Contracts
Correspondence To	Budgets	Operations
Correspondence From	Correspondence To	Correspondence To
Food and Beverage	Correspondence From	Correspondence From
Entertainment	Entertainment	Entertainment
Floral	Food and Beverage	Auction
Hotel	Operations	Venue
Floor Plans and Timelines	Miscellaneous	Budgets
Transportation		Notes
Budgets		Miscellaneous
Notes		
Miscellaneous		

Forming the Project Timeline

At this point you have a list of prospective venues and possible dates. Because you know when your event is and how it will flow and you have a general idea of where (or what kind of venue) it will be, you're ready to begin mapping your course and getting costs together. Charting your course is important for several reasons. By having a project timeline, you will have (1) a tool by which to measure your success, (2) a schedule by which you and your team will be able to complete tasks and meet deadlines, and (3) a reference tool that can be distributed easily to all your vendors.

The project timeline is a key element to staying organized. While your event timeline is the schedule for your guests' experience beginning at the start of the party, the project timeline begins now. You'll need a calendar and any information on the party you already may have. This includes all your notes on the venue, information on caterers or bands, and anything that is a part of your plan for this event.

Take your calendar and circle the date of your event. If a date isn't set yet, schedule it as beginning, middle, or end of the month. Your first step is to work backwards from that date. Calculate how many months, weeks, or days you have left to get this party planned. Give yourself a clean sheet of paper for each month (or if time is tight, a clean sheet for each week or each day), and start with what you know.

Whatever plans, deadlines, tasks, or responsibilities you have in place is where you'll begin, and then you'll work backwards. For example, if your event date is the beginning of October, you want guests to receive invitations six to eight weeks before the event date. Allowing one week for mailing will put you at a beginning-of-August deadline for mailing the invitations. If you want the envelopes addressed for you, find out from your calligrapher how much time she'll need to complete the job (the number of pieces and time of year will determine how long your calligrapher will require). Work backwards from your mailing date; add the calligraphy time (let's say two weeks for 75 invitations), and now the deadline for getting the invitations and addresses to the calligrapher is mid-July. Now ask your printer how long it takes to print the invitations (don't forget shipping time, and give yourself three days to go through and approve proofs). Add the printing time (one week for a standard invitation) to the calligraphy deadline, and now you have your deadline for ordering your invitations at the first week of July. Always give yourself cushion time, rounding out dates to allow for possible delays. This process of working backwards from when you need a task completed (from booking a keynote speaker to having flowers chosen and delivered to booking talent) applies to any task that is associated with the event. Don't be scared! We've included a general timeline that you can follow.

It's also important to insert all your personal deadlines. If you haven't chosen a venue or a date, insert a deadline by which you'll make that decision. Your venue also may place a deadline on you based on how long the managers will hold the space for you. If you're fluctuating between a dance band and a DJ, give yourself a deadline, and put it on the project timeline.

You will want to map out your monthly and weekly duties as well. When working with a team or committee, you will need to schedule regular meetings or conference calls. Insert these tasks on your timeline. In fact, your project timeline should be distributed among the team in order for everyone to keep up and choreograph everyone's efforts. Be thorough. Be detailed.

As a guideline, we put together a six-month project timeline that you can follow. Events (huge ones and small ones) are planned for years at a time, and sometimes they're planned in a matter of weeks. Six months is an average, but if you have less time, you'll want to combine tasks from one or more months. If you have more time than six months, you can distribute your tasks over a longer length of time. No matter how much time you have, you will still want to find potential venues, get a preliminary budget, and choose a date as soon as possible. The more time you have, the more choices you have for dates, venues, and vendors. Take advantage of it. The less time you have, the more limited you will be, so you'll want to complete those three key tasks right away to give yourself the best opportunity for success.

Sample Project Timeline

Six Months or More Before
- Pick a date.
- Put together your budget.
- Develop preliminary event timeline.
- Hold dates at several potential venues.
- Put together your guest list.
- Do creative development/brainstorming.
- Source your vendors (caterer, floral designer, photographer, rentals, printer, tenting, etc.).
- Source your entertainment.
- Put holds on (or reserve) all vendors that are chosen.
- Begin to gather/negotiate contracts.
- Determine any site logistics.
- Source your officiant (wedding).
- Find your wedding gown.

Four Months or More Before

- Contract all your vendors.
- Contract your entertainment.
- Refine budget.
- Refine event timeline.
- Determine equipment rental requirements.
- Determine in-house equipment available and any need for supplemental rentals (tables, chairs, linens, etc.).
- Initial venue meeting with contracted vendors.
- Choose your printed materials (save-the-date, invitation, program, etc.).
- Send out save-the-date reminders.
- Send out deposits.
- Begin menu planning.
- Research gift ideas and source vendor.
- Determine need for access credentials (laminated card, pin, ticket, etc.).
- Source hotel accommodations.
- Begin to arrange for ground transportation.

Two to Three Months or More Before

- Finalize menu.
- Finalize decor.
- Mail invitations.
- Finalize floor plans.
- Order credentials.
- All vendor contracts should be signed and deposits sent out.
- Refine budget.
- Finalize event timeline and send to all necessary vendors.
- Review staffing requirements (or staffing provided).
- Secure any necessary permits.
- Determine any signage (directional and otherwise) requirements.
- Begin first draft of program or remarks.
- Place rental order.
- Order rings (wedding).

One Month or More Before

- Do menu tasting.
- Finalize any menu changes and print menu card.
- Secure all basic technical arrangements.
- Formulate schedule for load-in/load-out.

- Request any necessary insurance certificates from vendors.
- Pinpoint initial security issues (if any).
- Review any last-minute issues with all vendors.
- Finalize second draft of program or remarks.
- Should receive all giveaways.
- Finalize and print event program.

Two Weeks Before
- Completed schedule for load-in/load-out.
- Send load-in/load-out schedule to all necessary vendors (including venue).
- Distribute schedules, logistics, and credentialing procedures to vendors, crew, and on-site staff.
- Send event timeline to all necessary vendors.
- Follow up with any guests who have not replied.
- Arrange for a venue walk-through with photographer, videographer, and any other necessary vendors.
- Do your seating arrangement.
- Apply for marriage license (wedding).
- Get final guest guarantee to caterer.
- Make any revisions to load-in/load-out schedule received by vendors.

One Week Before
- Follow up on any missing shipments (giveaways, flowers, décor, etc.).
- Assemble on-site event packet to include load-in/load-out schedule, event timeline, floor plan(s), contact list, and any specific logistics.
- Confirm arrival times with all vendors.
- Prepare balance payments.
- Arrange for all necessary event rehearsals.
- Make any revisions to seating plan.

Day of Event
- All key staff to be on site.
- Be sure to arrive *before* any vendors arrive.
- Touch base with venue contact.
- Distribute communications.
- Distribute credentials to staff and crew.
- All setup complete at least 30 minutes prior to guest arrival.
- All services (food, bars, valet, coat check, music, etc.) in place prior to guest arrival.

After the Event
- Send thank-you letters/notes.
- Generate final budget.
- Send out any overage payments.

Finding Vendors

Your next step in creating your event blueprint is to research the various suppliers you could use (because *vendor* is the most widely used and accepted term for supplier in this industry, you'll want to get comfortable using it from now on). It is so important to develop relationships with your vendors. They are your source of expert advice. This is not to say that you should accept their terms as gospel. Think of choosing your vendors as picking your team. You will all be working together to reach one goal, and that goal is to pull off a successful event.

The first step is to find some vendors for your various needs. You likely will need separate vendors for your food, your equipment, your flowers, or any other specific need of your party. How do you find vendors? And most important, how do you choose the one that's best for your event?

It can be nerve-wracking to work with and trust someone new. The good news is that there are ways to find good people without resorting to closing your eyes and pointing to entries in the phone book.

- *Keep your eyes and ears open.* When you attend parties, go out to dinner, go window shopping, and so on, take note of the things you loved. If the food was outstanding at your company holiday party, ask for the name of the caterer. If the dance band was fabulous at your niece's wedding, get the bandleader's card. If the flowers at your favorite restaurant are always fresh and gorgeous, ask the manager for the florist's name and number. Inspiration comes in all forms, but you'll only find it if you're looking.
- *Hotels.* If you just can't find a good florist, call the nicest hotel in town (or close to town) and ask the concierge to tell you who does the hotel's flowers. The hotel's banquets department also will have a good line on photographers, linen houses, and even a dependable minister, rabbi, or priest.
- *Other vendors.* Let's say that you love your caterer but have no idea who to use for floral design. Ask your caterer, whose judgment you already know you trust! Not only will your caterer probably know several florists, but he also should have a good sense of your style.

- *Publications.* The phone book and the Internet are good places to start sourcing vendors. Also, social magazines such as *InStyle, Los Angeles, Chicago,* and so on run stories on parties in every issue. If you see something you like, do the research. If the article doesn't list the supplier, call the venue where the party was held, get to the person in charge, and ask her for the lead. Be resourceful! Even though these parties are for the rich and famous, not every one of their clients is a celebrity. In addition, (1) a good vendor will work within your budget, and (2) if he can't, he will be very forthcoming with you, and (3) most likely will refer you to someone who can work on your event. We have found many wonderful vendors this way. Be encouraged!
- *Research.* Once you've found someone, get the information on that person. Check out her Web site and call her references. You also may want to ask if you can pop into an event that person is currently working on so that you can see how her staff is conducted on site. In addition, it's good to see something in person rather than in a photograph or on video.
- *Comparisons.* The key factor in comparing vendor quotes is to make sure it's apples to apples. Each quote should include the same thing. For example, if shipping is included on one, be sure it's included on the other. You also want to be up-front with your vendors and let them know that you are obtaining quotes from other companies. At the same time, you are not obligated to tell them who these companies are.
- *Be honest.* When you have chosen your "team," you should phone any vendors you have not chosen. At this time we generally do tell them whom we have chosen. And we always give a reason, but be constructive. Maybe your styles didn't match, or maybe the vendor didn't fit the budget, or the other company was better prepared with a presentation. Be honest and constructive; it makes everyone better at what they do.
- *Like your team.* All things being equal, we like to go with the person that we most strongly believe we'll enjoy working with. Planning an event can be emotionally draining, and the hours you spend with your vendors can be long, start early in the morning, and end in the middle of the night. Those hours go by much easier when you get along with your vendors and enjoy a solid working relationship.

As you narrow down your list of vendors to your final choice, be sure to ask questions so that you can adequately compare one vendor with another. The following questions are key to ask in any vendor situation:

- What are your payment terms?
- What is included in my contract?
- Who is included in my contract (staffing)?
- What do you charge for overtime?
- What sort of requirements do you have?
- What do I need to supply?
- Who will be on site?
- Is there a charge for delivery? For setup? For tear-down?
- How much time will you need to set up? To tear down?
- At what time will you (your equipment, staff, etc.) arrive on site?
- Can you provide a certificate of insurance?

Your vendors also will be able to give you all the answers you will need to fill in your project timeline. They will supply you with a variety of deadlines, including

- Contract deadline/signature
- Payment schedule and terms
- Vendor requirements (power supply, equipment, etc.)
- Design choices
- Layout decisions (floor plans)
- Load-in times

Schedule the deadlines on your timeline to make sure that they align with all your other responsibilities. As you begin working with your team, your conversations will produce a domino effect of decisions and deadlines to be made. The only way to keep track of all of them is to plot them out on your project timeline.

Your project timeline, just as your budget, is a work in progress. It will change, it will get longer, but it stills keeps everyone on the same page. Think of it as your benchmark of sanity.

Sanity doesn't always come easy. Your best chance for keeping sane is to keep organized. Over the course of planning your event, you will need to make so many choices, scale hurdles, and be an effective problem solver. Having an event book where you can store your notes and maintain contracts and correspondence will make it easier. Remember, you're not just managing your success but also the performance of your vendors. Their success will depend on your project timeline marking critical tasks and keeping everyone in forward motion toward the goal of a successful event.

EVENT SUCCESS STORY:
FUNDRAISING GALA ON A *TIGHT* SCHEDULE

We usually like to have at least six months to plan a major event, but sometimes you don't have that luxury. We have had clients come to us at the eleventh hour to plan a variety of different events. The one that stands out in our memory was when our receptionist informed us that Elizabeth Taylor's assistant was on the phone. We had been recommended by Cirque du Soleil to handle the event management and fill the 2,500 seats of the Big Top for their opening night benefit performance in Chicago. Additionally, we were charged with creating a pre and post party for 500 VIP guests of the Elizabeth Taylor AIDS Foundation, determining the best local charities to be the beneficiaries, soliciting celebrity attendance and involvement, and handling all the operations and logistics.

The crazy part was that we had only six weeks to plan the event, design and mail invitations, create a buzz, research venue locations for the post event, send celebrity letters, and as assist in raising funds. We decided it would be in everyone's best interest if we had several local AIDS beneficiaries combining their efforts to raise the funds as well as attend such a high-profile event. Celebrities attending included Oprah Winfrey, Woody Harrelson, Otis Wilson, Rosie O'Donnell, former Senator Carol Moseley-Braun, Oliver Stone, and of course, Elizabeth Taylor.

It began with the design of the invitations, venue selection, setting up the RSVP line, catering, and how to entertain the guests in a special way because the Cirque performers all were going to attend the post party. We spent long hours fielding questions about whether Liz Taylor herself actually would attend, where the tickets were located, and how close would they be to the performance. By the end of the six weeks, we were so fluent in the ticketing/seating of the Big Top that the Cirque staff asked us if we would travel with them.

The Elizabeth Taylor/Cirque du Soleil event was an incredible success that raised over $150,000 for local AIDS centers, received enormous publicity, and brought a great deal of excitement to opening night.

Cirque performers welcome the guests for opening night. *(Matthew Kaplan Photography.)*

EVENT SUCCESS STORY:
PLAN IN ADVANCE FOR BIG EVENTS

For the Olympics in Atlanta, our planning began 16 months in advance with regular conference calls, weekly progress reports, entertainment schedules, and a three-day trip to Atlanta every other week. The organizational process began with just a simple three-inch binder that mushroomed into a five-inch binder, and when we were ready to go on site 16 months later, we had individual binders for each of the six venues as well as two five-inch binders filled with contracts, correspondence, entertainment schedules, entertainment riders, production information, and lots of ticketing requests.

The center of the athlete village—Summer Olympic Games, Atlanta, GA, 1996. *(PWEE Staff.)*

A project of this size and magnitude required our best effort in managing the details. We had meetings with every department of the Atlanta Committee for the Olympic Games, including ticketing, to accommodate any actual event ticket requests, food and beverage to provide all the catering for the artists and their entourage for both dinner and backstage hospitality, travel to handle air, transportation to handle ground needs, housing for accommodations and security for ingress and egress of performers, the credentialing process, the alcohol and drug policies of the village, as well as general security for the acts.

Managing all the details and needs for one performer or one venue is time-consuming in and of itself; artist riders are filled with lots of things that can be construed as insignificant or trivial to an outsider (such as a bowl of green M&Ms, tube socks and boxers, or grilled chicken on Tuesdays). When you multiply this by 250 different performers in six different venues, the process could become overwhelming. If one item that is really important to the band is missing; they could choose not to perform. Thankfully, this has never happened. But it could. . . .

The next part of our logistical challenges was the extensive amount, and different types of security guarding the borders of the athlete village. We worked closely with Olympic security to create a plan that would allow for the easiest access to the village for the entertainers while still maintaining the safety and integrity of the village. Security at the Olympic Games is comprised of many of the best security agencies from around the world; agencies from the FBI to Interpol to the Masaad. Their primary function is to protect the athletes while inside the village and maintaining the village borders. Therefore, bringing in rock stars who do not want to share their real name or choose not to use a last name became very trying for all involved.

The babysitting process was even more challenging because no one could enter or move freely inside the village without an accredited escort at all times. Over the course of 33 days, we did manage to develop and implement a process that was fairly painless and got the entertainers to their venues on time to rehearse and perform.

Hootie & The Blowfish performs at Georgia Tech Stadium. *(PWEE Staff.)*

Tips for Organized Success

- *Learn the language.* We all know the adage, "When in Rome. . . ." Negotiating with vendors and venues will be easier if you speak the same language and can follow along in conversation. Here are some terms that you will hear and use frequently. For example, suppliers are *vendors,* and linens are *dropped* on tables. Appendix B provides definitions for some of the most common phrases and vocabulary in the event-planning industry.
- *Pad your deadlines.* One of the best ways to stay in budget, save money, and protect your sanity is to allow for plenty of time and for plenty of mistakes. For example, when you schedule times for shipment deliveries (such as your giveaways or printed materials), allot a few extra days for any delays that might occur.
- *Get it in writing.* Whether it's the number of centerpieces, the arrival time of the DJ, a fee waiver at your venue, or proof of insurance—put it in the contract, get it in a letter, or print the e-mail. Have all deliverables that are promised to you in writing and on hand.
- *Be proactive.* As you go through your production, it's always smart to address potential issues as well as existing issues. For example, ask your venue contact how load-in usually runs. We've had venues where there is only one bank of elevators to get to the ballroom. That means that all our vendors had to load in their equipment, decor, linens, and crew along with any other guests of the venue. We asked for a dedicated elevator for setup and teardown. This minimized our union labor hours and helped us stay in budget. Don't just hope for the best. Be proactive and create your own best situation.
- *Be updated.* Managing an event requires you to take the lead. Be aware of everyone's deadlines, not just your own. Staying organized by updating your project timeline will help you to lead your vendors and your team to meet all your project milestones.

Budgeting the Event

Your Budget Is a Work in Progress

Putting together a budget can be a bit like solving a mystery. The answer to one question always seems to lead you to other questions, the answers to which them-

EVENT SUCCESS STORY: MANAGING MULTIPLE EVENTS FOR A SINGLE CLIENT

We have been involved in a lot of unusual scenarios, but few events come close to the excitement of handling grand openings in multiple cities filled with athletes and celebrities. In each city we created the ultimate event outside for the public featuring a sports festival during the day, a competition of the greatest sports team in history, concerts, and the top 20 athletes of the sports century. The motorcade to the VIP party began with a professional football marching band and cheerleaders followed by a motorcade of 25 limousines filled with celebrities and athletes. The finale included a mascot running down the main artery of the city holding the ceremonial sports kabob of the entertainment venue, which then was followed by a fireworks blast from the top of the building. The inside entertainment also featured concerts by name talent. We had a grand opening plan that worked and that needed to be tweaked slightly for each city, but we had it all together.

Red carpet arrivals in Times Square. *(PWEE Staff.)*

For one opening, we were in New York City with thousands of people lining the streets of Times Square. We had some of the top athletes of the sports century and film and television celebrities walking the red carpet, and just as the outside production was about to begin, on live TV, the director got on the radio and asked where the ceremonial kabob was, because we were just about ready to cue the kabob to be raised to signal the fireworks. No one seemed to know its location; the client had it last. But it doesn't matter how it happened; it had to be found because we had already started the live feed!

(Continued)

The hunt was on. All our team members split up and began a search and rescue effort for the missing kabob. One member of our team started digging through the offices and found the lost item in a box buried in a closet in someone's office. Tick Tock. We had three minutes to hand off the kabob to the show host; and so the race began. Down three flights of stairs through the VIP guests who had already made their way into the building and then handing off the kabob in Olympic relay race fashion to the next person who had to make his way through the throng of people to get backstage in time for the finale. We had our emcee stretch his remarks/interviews and survived the craziness yet again unscathed.

Chris Berman and Stuart Scott hold up the kabob as the kickoff to the fireworks. *(PWEE Staff.)*

selves provoke yet more questions. Stay organized, informed, and energetic, and your preliminary budget will be close to your final budget. To help you on your way, we've assembled a general budget sheet. Add in and take out line items to tailor it to your specific needs, making sure that your budget is thorough—and don't forget the tax!

Budgeting is much more layered than plugging in numbers and adding them up. Your creativity comes into play in every facet of event production, including staying in budget. But you also must understand that an event's budget is a working document that will not be final until your event is over. In order to keep your budget from spinning out of control, however, you have to learn some of the basics of budget management. The three main aspects of budget management are *research*, *negotiation,* and *creative money allocation.*

Research for your event is twofold. First, you need to do your homework on the vendors you are choosing. Make sure that they are qualified and have the experience you're going to require for your event. (Check out the section in this chapter called "Finding Vendors.") Follow up with their references. Check their Web sites. Attend an event that they are working on. Second, make sure that what you're getting is what you're paying for. Avoid surprises later by researching your contracts. Here are some sample questions to ask as you do your research:

- Do they include tax?
- Do they include gratuity?
- Do they include labor?
- Is the time allotted in the contract enough time for the vendor to complete the job, or will there be overtime?
- Do you have to supply anything?

The questions in the preceding section on choosing vendors will go a long way toward getting all the information you need.

The art of negotiation with vendors and venues is simply one way to find alternative means to get the same result or at least the same effect. Negotiation is a give-and-take process between your ideas and what is possible. Getting proposals and quotes from vendors is the first step in that process. Remember, you don't always have to accept first proposals, but on the other hand, you don't always have to find alternative vendors. If you've found someone with whom you really want to work, encourage him to massage the budget. Have him give suggestions on where he can trim his budget to fit within yours.

If after you've filled in your line items on your budget sheet and the estimated total is more than you thought, you now need to apply some creative money allocation. So many times we've put together a budget just to realize that one line item was more than we originally thought. Most times we can just move the dollars around and still be within the bottom-line number. When that fails, we refer back to the five *W*s. What is crucial to this party? Is it the entertainment? Is it the location? You may need to scale back on one or more other, less crucial line items to achieve your overall goal for a successful event. Of course, only you know the key elements of the event, but you should focus on those and then do a little research or negotiate a little more to get some other line items within your final number.

What follows is a sample budget that is actually a hybrid of many events that we've done. In other words, it can work for any type of event, whether it's for an office function, a private party, or even a charity fund-raiser. This sample budget is a way to help you organize your line items even though your event might end up a much simpler affair than what this sample budget implies. We've added almost every possible expense we could think of to this list to help you cover all your bases and keep you from forgetting something. Most event budgets will not have all these line items. There aren't any steadfast rules or line items that you must have in your event budget. Each one is different from the last, so use this list as a guideline, and make it work for you. Take note of the "Show Production" section of the budget. This is strictly if you plan to hire name talent. While we strongly recommend that a professional be hired if your event calls for name talent, we think it's valuable to at least be familiar with the general costs associated with a show production. Definitions of the industry terms used in this section also can be found in Appendix B.

Sample Budget Line Items

Venue Charges
- Rental fee
- Fee for additional hours needed
- Labor (maintenance staff, building engineer, electricians, stagehands)
- Security
- Valet service
- Bathroom attendants
- Elevator attendants
- Cleanup crew
- Power charges

Food and Beverage
- Menu package
- Wines and champagne
- Cake (for birthdays, weddings, new company launches, anniversaries, etc.)

Decor
- Linens, napkins, napkin rings, and chair covers
- Floral (entrance piece, escort card table, food stations, bathrooms, centerpieces, etc.)
- Specialty/atmosphere lighting

- Floral camouflage screens (to hide unsightly exit doors, service entrances, etc.)
- Fabric swagging (tent ceilings, service entrances, sound board tables, etc.)

Incidental Entertainment
- Strings group to greet guests
- Cocktail music
- Dinner music
- Dance band
- Postevent quartet
- Roving entertainment
- Emcee

Show Production
- Talent performance fee
- Sound, lighting, and union labor
- Custom staging
- Backdrop
- Hospitality
- Backline equipment
- Ground transportation
- Hotel accommodations
- Airfares
- Piano tuner

Equipment Rentals
- Chairs (chivari, wood-padded, opera, garden, etc.)
- Tables (rounds, banquets)
- Flatware or silver
- Glassware or crystal
- Specialty plate chargers and matching glassware
- Tiered silver dessert trays
- Bathroom tables
- Tables for furniture groupings
- Sofas for furniture groupings

Tenting
- Main tent
- Kitchen tent

73

- Valet or drive-through tent
- Entrance canopy
- Canopy walkway
- Flooring and carpet
- Permits
- Temperature control (heating or air-conditioning units)
- Portable power (generators)

Materials

- Merge and purge service
- Fulfillment and assembly service
- Save-the-date mailer
- Invitations
- Escort cards, place cards, and table numbers
- Menu cards
- Programs
- Calligraphy
- Postage

Sound, Staging, Lighting, and Labor

- Sound and lighting equipment rental
- Staging rental
- Labor (for load-in, install, run, and tear-down of equipment)
- Video projection

Transportation

- Limousines
- Buses/minibuses
- Drivers
- Dispatch person

Miscellaneous

- Photographer
- Film buyout for negatives
- Videographer
- Video edit
- Greeters and people movers
- Staffing
- Communications

- Executive bathrooms
- Mobile dressing rooms
- Guest amenities (in rooms)
- Bathroom amenities
- Giveaways
- Signage
- Insurance
- Tuxedo rentals (for staff and security)
- Officiant
- Gratuities
- 10 percent contingency

Tips for Budgeting Success

We've found that there are many secrets to creating a successful event budget. Keep these successful ideas in mind as you put together your own budget:

- *Source good vendors.* Having a good vendor translates to an experienced team, translates to quality service and products, and translates to a successful event.
- *Check your contracts.* We all know this to be beneficial, but it's a good reminder. Pay special attention to your event date listed on the contract, as well as load-in and load-out times. You won't want a vendor to accidentally double book your date or show up too late on event day.
- *Be flexible.* Be firm on what's most important, but know when to bend in order to meet your goals. The most cost-effective things to be flexible on are the event date (Fridays and Sundays have lower food and beverage minimums than Saturdays; the same goes for afternoon versus evening events) and the menu (think fewer courses, no champagne, or arranging to supply your own bar).
- *Allow for plenty of time.* Don't get caught with rush charges and late fees. Plan ahead for usual delays (mailing or shipping), and pay your vendors on time.
- *Don't forget the tax.* Find the bottom-line number on your contracts. If you're not sure if tax is charged, ask. If you can't get an answer, add it in yourself to be safe. Also, in some states the gratuity charged is taxable, which will affect your bottom line. Another tax that is easy to forget is the hotel room tax. When you get room rates, ask for the room rate including tax.

**EVENT SUCCESS STORY:
KNOW WHERE YOU MIGHT ENCOUNTER ADDITIONAL EXPENSES**

We are very protective of a client's budget because management of the finances is how we have managed to develop long-term relationships over the years. Many times we will even estimate on the high side on a particular line item to make sure that we stay within the budget to the end. There is only one variable that can put a wrench in this concept, and that is union labor. When working in a union venue, you can only estimate to the best of your abilities, and sometimes your guess can be off. The chances of having a line item be wrong are very slim, but if and when it does happen, it usually involves producing name acts.

We produced a tenth anniversary gala for a charity client at the beautiful Navy Pier ballroom in Chicago with name talent. We negotiated with the agent and the production manager about the specifics of what we absolutely had to provide for the artist to not compromise the show (sound, lighting, video, backline equipment, labor call, etc.), but keeping the goal of the event in mind (making money for the charity).

Once we finalized the details, we began planning the load-in schedule with the union labor needs for the setup, the event itself, and tear-down. The guests didn't move to dinner as quickly as we would have liked because they were still bidding on items in the auction, which meant more money for the organization, and dinner service took longer than we had planned. The bottom line was that we were over an hour behind for the headliner to perform, and the act decided to do a few more minutes than we had originally contracted, which normally would have been fantastic, but in this case it just compounded our already growing labor bill.

Go over eight hours, you've moved into the hugely expensive world of overtime. But when your event is on a Saturday night and you go over eight hours into Sunday morning, you are looking at double time, which was not figured into the budget. This was something we had prepared the client for in advance as a possibility, based on the budget and how careful we had to be with the dollars, but something that seemed to go in one ear and out the other, leaving lots of confusion on how the budget grew exponentially. We worked through the details, and the event ended up raising more than double the amount of money from the year before because of the entertainment, so everything worked out in the end. But the lesson learned is that you should always be prepared for the worst and communicate your concerns in order to make the event perfect.

- *Focus on key elements.* Don't forget those five *W*s! Know what's most important so that you can trim the superfluous.
- *Update it frequently.* You might want to keep a column of budgeted amounts and actual amounts. This will help you to keep track of what you're truly spending.

- *Know possible overages.* Know ahead of time what overtime costs you will incur if you decide to extend the time of the event. Making informed decisions helps to keep you in budget.
- *Give yourself a 10 percent contingency.* If you add 10 percent of your budget to the bottom line, you will either financially prepare yourself for possible mistakes, rush charges, or overtime, or you will be pleasantly surprised when you come in under budget.

4

Step Four:
Design Your Event

Designing the creative treatment for parties is probably our favorite part of event production (except maybe the dessert tastings). This part *can* be the most fun because it's very creative. It *can* be challenging because what you want to do may not always be possible. One thing designing the creative treatment will do is stretch your problem-solving abilities.

Designing the event goes way beyond what the room looks like. Designing your event will require that you harvest your inspiration from many places. Inspiration can be in the fabric, the flowers, the space, or the time of year. Wherever you find it, when you do draft your event, remember to design *your entire event*. What we mean by this is to create a thread that will weave your event from the beginning (the invitation) to the end (valet pickup) and after (thank-you notes). It should all work together cohesively, building a full experience. This thread we speak of can be a color, the elegant atmosphere, a fun theme, the tapas menu, the interactive entertainment, or the worthy cause. Find the thread that works for you, and then communicate it through your printed materials, your decor design, your menu, the guest experience, everything. This is our best tip for well-designed event success.

80

Using Harley "Hogs" is an obvious decor choice for a Harley motorcycle theme party, but hanging them as sculptures is a fun twist. *(PWEE Staff.)*

Pull the Look Together

What is decor? And how do you choose and use it? These are rudimentary questions, but decor may be a lot more than you think. Decor is many things, but there are two steadfast rules. Be consistent, and use your space. Your look should be reflected in the flowers, linens, decor, and even your menu and entertainment.

This benefit gala for Project Exploration is a good example of using your cause as your decor. The big challenge was assembling the Jobaria dinosaurs correctly! *(John Reilly Photography.)*

We usually avoid themes that are too "theme-y." For example, if you wanted to do a casino night and create an atmosphere like a Club Havana, the room still would have the casino tables but you wouldn't necessarily need a sign that read, "Casino Night." Convey your message, your theme, with furniture groupings in rich fabrics, lounge waitresses in costume, huge fans on the ceiling, and maybe a salsa band with dancers. The idea is to not hit your guests over the head with the name of the party. Create a look that does the talking for you.

Using your space means finding elements that are proportionate to your space. A venue with 30-foot ceilings will need large, "impactful" pieces that won't get lost. On the other hand, a venue with a 10-foot ceiling requires shorter, fuller centerpieces. With your space in mind and your setting coming together, where should you start?

Flowers

Flowers are always a good place to get started. They also can spark inspiration. Flowers are a good place to spend your money not only because they give your party color,

EVENT SUCCESS STORY:
TYING TOGETHER ELEMENTS FOR AN ELEGANT LANDSCAPE

For the grand opening of a major resort and casino in Atlantic City, we were asked to put together a series of parties that were elegant and elaborate. The challenge was to whip up an elaborate event without overshadowing the main focus of the event—the property itself. As we designed the events it was important to communicate the casino's essence through the decor and entertainment. The entire environment was tied together with collective design details. The lobby bars were echoed within the tablescape designs, and the stage decor resonated in the features of the chairs, and so on. This environment of high design combining the clean lines of Armani with the excitement of Atlantic City's newest resort property.

The grand opening concept was a series of events over four weekends. While each weekend would have the same "look," each was kept unique from the others—through the use of flowers, lighting, and entertainment.

The first locale in this high-style scene was the reception in the foyer, where all five senses were titillated. Spanning from the floor to 12 feet high, four custom floor lamps creating dramatic silhouettes gave a hint of what was inside the ballroom. Soft lighting and strumming sounds set the mood, with fragrant flowers and candles on the cocktail tables, along with stunning floral designed for the food stations.

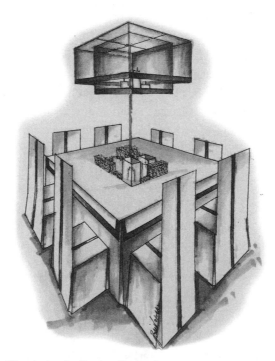

Tablescape design. *(Rendering by Design Fusion.)*

Emulating the essence of a fabulous dinner party, we set the ballroom with square tables of eight. The table linens and chair covers were finished in incredible muslin fabrics trimmed in satin and floral designs created specially for this event. The table setting was decorated with framed flats of wheat grass and mosses accented with six arrangements of pavé rose clusters. For a dramatic effect and to highlight the textural features of the tables, a custom lampshade extended six feet high from the mixed design of candles to cast a soft glow. We set a pin spot on each table as well. Wash luminaries bathed the ballroom walls and ceiling with subtle color and artistic projections.

Each week, the tablescapes varied in style and color. One week we used round mounds of tightly arranged floral groups, all in deep, rich red flowers (roses, dahlias, etc.), whereas the next week there was a mixture of bamboo vases and bamboo-wrapped candles with a Zen palate that included green mosses, white pebble stones, bamboo stalks, and cymbidium orchids.

The next visual experience was the stage. It too possessed a bold design in which the details were key. Large scenic shapes were covered in a neutral but fairly rough texture and finished with a darker band on the side panels. These panels changed often with stage lighting, and the texture intensified with a change of direction. The panels were on full-stage traveler tracks to achieve at least 12 different looks and 24 ground plans. The scenery was as flexible as you would see on any of the big award shows.

The backdrop and the overhead "headers" all were created based on the same concept—a mixture of textured walls and translucent mottled bands. We were able to lower and raise the headers, giving the ability to iris down or open up the space to frame or to back a performer and, of course, allowing for a multitude of different ways to light the stage dramatically.

Overall ballroom. *(Sheri Whitko Photography.)*

Only a highly elaborate location with marble walls and a 10-foot cast-stone fireplace could accommodate a floral tree such as this one. *(John Reilly Photography.)*

84

life, and an incredible aroma but also because there are so many to choose from that they can represent anything from casual to formal to silly. You'll want to choose flowers and a floral design that communicates the atmosphere you are creating.

- Is your event black tie formal? Think Casablanca lilies, roses, and big dahlias.

- Is it outdoor casual? Think peonies, lisianthus, and bright gerbera daisies.
- Is this a business setting? Think small, compact arrangements in muted colors.

If you're overwhelmed, narrow your choices. Go with only flowers that are in season. Or choose from locally grown flowers. If you don't need to import flowers, they will be less expensive. But the opposite can be so much fun. You can get your hands on almost any flower at almost any time of year.

Finding a good floral designer is key. This person will either help you define your look or will interpret what you've already put together. Depending on what the flowers are and how they are arranged, you can communicate an endless range of looks. Flowers also go lots of places other than on your tables. They go on food stations; they make fantastic, impressive entrance pieces; and they're perfect in bathrooms and at coat check booths. Look to put them on mantles, on countertops, and at place settings.

Another thing to consider with flowers is the container. A one-of-a-kind container will be significantly more expensive than a stock container. Also, you don't always *need* a container, especially for your centerpieces. Your floral designer can create a centerpiece that rests in a plain green plastic tray and then arrange the flowers to overflow and cover the ugly green. Instant savings!

To complement the high design of a hotel property, a clean Zen look was created for the centerpieces. *(Sheri Whitko Photography.)*

Your container choices will depend on what your floral designer has in stock. Or, for example, your venue may have containers that you could embellish. You'll want to work with your designer's inventory and your venue's existing decor, or you may even want to provide some of your own. Floral arrangements can be created in anything from a basket, bowl, vase, or plate or attached to branches, entryways, hearths, or doors.

Remember that you're paying not only for the flowers and materials but also for your designer's time and creativity, as well as the labor to make the arrangements. If your budget does not have a lot of room for elaborate floral arrangements, go with in-season stems, in-stock inventory for your containers, and simply done arrangements that don't require a lot of labor.

Linens

Linens range from the average (rainbow of usual colors in the poly-cotton blends) to the fabulous (beaded organza, raw silk, and gorgeous patterns). With that comes the wide range of rental prices. Linens should underscore your design. They can bring it all together for you. With the flowers, the right lighting, and the right serving platters and place settings, the linens can make a real statement. With a less flexible budget, you can get away with less.

With linens we follow one hard-line rule. They *always must* go to the floor. You can rent the most gorgeous linens, and if they don't go to the floor, you might as well have not spent the money because every rented table (even tables that hotels keep in their inventory) has ugly metal legs. To complete your look, and if you can work it into your budget, you'll want to cover those legs. Some venues (particularly hotels) will try to tell you that doing two squares on a round table to make an "eight-point linen" is good enough. They're right—it *just* passes. If you must draw the budget line there, then so be it. If you can, rent a *round* linen for a *round* table and a *banquet* linen for a *banquet* table. To reference all the table and linens sizes, you can check out Appendix B.

Another way to cut corners is to use in-house linens for your food stations and bars and then rent linens just for your dining and cocktail tables. Or you can choose lower-end linens (such as a poly-cotton blend solid or a simple imperial stripe) for all of your tables and then hopefully have enough budget room to do all the tables. The best way to know where to cut corners is to figure out where your guests will spend most of their time. For example, the cocktail hour can be very short, but your guests could spend most of the evening at the dinner rounds. Avoid costly boutique linens for the cocktail tables by using in-house linens, and then rent high-end linens for the dinner rounds.

86

With an ample budget, custom linens can convey a look of lavishness and elegance. To complete the environment, the right lighting has to be implemented as well. *(John Reilly Photography.)*

Make sure that you stay with neutral colors for those in-house linens. You don't want them to compete with your other decor. In hotels you'll find a lot of dusty rose, pale greens, and colors that usually match the busy ballroom carpets. Black, white, and ivory are the best, safest colors because they either disappear in the room or will coordinate with other linens that you may have brought in.

Lighting

Lighting is decor. There is a difference between stage lighting and atmosphere lighting, and if you remember, we break out these two numbers in our budgets in Chapter 3. We use atmosphere lighting to pin spot or highlight the food stations, centerpieces, sculptures, and space detail. We also use atmosphere lighting on fabrics so that we can change the mood during the course of the party. Atmosphere

When you're able to take in the entire surroundings of an event, you are able to see how important it is for the linens to go to the floor. *(John Reilly Photography.)*

It was important to keep the stately feel of this presidential library when illuminating the building
for its grand opening ceremony. *(John Reilly Photography.)*

This is a good example of the use of lighting as decor in order to transform the raw environment into an inviting space to entice potential tenants and retailers. *(Matthew Kaplan Photography.)*

lighting can be quite expensive, and you need a reliable professional to help you with the logistics. In a large space, though, such as a big tent, a warehouse, or a room with very high ceilings and plain walls, atmosphere lighting can be a cost-effective, high-impact decor element.

What's fun about lighting are the colors to choose from and the patterns. There are "intelligent" lights that can change position, color, and pattern with the touch of a button. There are "can" lights that can highlight a painted ceiling or give an amber wash to a small stage. Then there are "gobos," which are plates that can be customized for your party and then placed on a fixture to shine a company name, event name, or interesting graphic shape. Be sure to work with a lighting company that specializes in special events because these companies are familiar with the specific needs for parties (as opposed to concert tours). Another way to enhance your ambient lighting is to use candles on your tables. Candles are a nice, generally inexpensive way to add a glow to a small area, and they make your guests look great! Always check with your venue for any open flame rules, but we always like to put candles (even if it's just a few votive candles) on the tables.

Aside from lighting as decor, you also have general area lighting. This type of workhorse lighting simply illuminates the space so that guests can make their way around. General area lighting is usually focused on pathways to make them safer and on food stations so that guests can see the food.

Fabric

Fabric makes wonderful decor. You can drape it, stretch it, light it, customize it, tie it, and shape it. Fabric can enhance a space, create a backdrop for video, camouflage an ugly wall, wrap poles, and create hallways. It comes in every color and design, and when in a pinch, it can dress up a space in no time at all. Our favorite place to find fabric is at a fabric mart. If your city doesn't have one, even just going to a fabric store can be a wonderful resource. If your decor plans require more than just a few bolts of fabric (say, to drape a wall), you'll need your decor vendor to get the fabric for you. Also, if you are using the fabric to cover tent poles, your tenting company also could provide the fabric and install it as well.

Be Creative and Resourceful

Sculptures, paintings, stage sets, trees, plants, flooring, furniture groupings, and fabric are all examples of the customary decor ideas that you see. Finding the resources for this type of decor is fairly easy. Sometimes your venue already will have artwork or sculptures, in which case you should use those types of things to your advantage and work them into your design. Other items such as trees and plants are as close as the nearest nursery. One alternative to buying plants (such as orchid plants as a centerpiece or palm trees at a tropical event) is to rent them. There are companies that rent plants and trees, but you also can make that request at the local nursery.

90

If you have a large space that needs to feel fuller, furniture groupings are a wonderful way to add to your design and provide seating as well. Sometimes a sea of cocktail tables can be bland or commonplace. Furniture groupings bring in another design element that is functional as well. Furniture also can be rented. To find a furniture rental company, simply check the Internet or even the Yellow Pages.

Along with these decor choices, what you may not know is that animals (camels at an Aladdin party or aquariums of fish built into a custom bar), people (interactive characters or painted models dripping in jewelry), and artisans (tile makers at a Mexican fiesta or a perched mermaid on a seafood station) all can be considered living decor. Your only limits are your imagination and your budget.

EVENT SUCCESS STORY: THINKING OUTSIDE THE BOX

Instead of doing a traditional ribbon cutting, we had wanted to do an unzipping for a mall opening where the front of the building was "wrapped" in fabric, and *unzipped*. We finally got our chance to do this for a retail property outside of Chicago. Our concept called for a huge zipper at the main entrance of this facade instead of a large ribbon and bow. The special program and our stunt would begin with the extraordinary *unzipping* of the building. The music builds to a crescendo, the pyro bursts begin with CO_2 jet blasts, and the confetti cannons explode over the crowd to start off the grand opening with a bang, and give the newspapers something to photograph.

We had pitched this concept to many clients, and we were so excited that we finally were going to have an opportunity to bring this unique ribbon cutting to fruition. We had the display custom made, and the designer came in for the event. It looked amazing. We set everything up at the main entrance to the mall the day before, and the client was excited about the buzz it had already created with the media.

The next morning, the winds started to pick up about an hour before the ceremony was scheduled. All the key executives, dignitaries, and media were beginning to gather when our unzipping wall started to become a sail. We did a test run of the zipper to make sure that everything would work perfectly, and during the rezipping process, a huge gust of wind came through and caused a snag within the actual zipper inside this giant zipper at the very top. Therefore, while everyone was sitting in his or her seats ready to begin, the designer determined that we needed to bring in a scissor lift to fix the zipper. Meanwhile, our entire team was behind the zipper (backstage) on the ground holding the piece together to avoid it from blowing open and ruining the surprise of the 100 piece marching band that was to kick off

the grand opening immediately following the ceremony. The designer pulled up on a scissor lift that made it seem like part of the program, because it was already planned to have the key executives do the unveiling of the new property from a lift. We fixed the malfunction, and the day continued with a perfect celebration, and the client, the crowd, and the media never knew the nightmare we escaped.

Instead of a ribbon cutting, this shopping mall hosted a grand "unzipping" with an appropriately large zipper instead of the traditional ribbon. *(PWEE Staff.)*

In one of the entertainment venues in the Athlete Village for the 1996 Olympic Games, the stage set of an original painting served as the feature decor fronting groups such as Run DMC. *(PWEE Staff.)*

Design is also in the *small things*. Don't forget the little areas that can leave big impressions. Beautiful flowers and matching linens on the escort card table are a nice touch. If the escort card table is outside, in the wind, find a clever way to anchor the cards, such as small river rocks or miniature paperweights. The bars are so utilitarian that it's always nice to find a way to make your guests remember them. Coordinate the linens, or since a floral arrangement could get in the way, you could put out a handsome bowl of extra large cashews or chocolate-covered raisins. Other guest stops such as the valet counter (small cookies to go) or the coat check (mints) are also nice places to "remind" your guests of the party.

Of all the small things not to forget, you must address the restrooms. Add your own decor of flowers, guest towels, or a convenience basket in the women's restroom. Is the bathroom old and a little dingy? Baskets of potpourri and sprinkled potpourri on the counters will clear that smell right up.

Questions to Ask

- What does your venue allow? Does it require covered flames? No confetti? Are you allowed to attach things to the walls? Do they allow indoor pyro?

- Have you accounted for labor in your budget—trucking, delivery, setup, tear-down?
- Have you made arrangements for postevent? Who is picking up leftover items, and when? Ask if the venue can store the vases, fabrics, or sculptures until the next business day so that you won't have to pay extra for late-night pickup.
- Has your decor person done a similar job like yours before? If she has, that's great because she has experience working with specific materials, but it's also not great because someone has done a similar look before.
- How much space will your decor take up? You'll need a footprint of the items so that you can map them out, whether they're on the floor, on tables, or on food stations.
- How high are your centerpieces? They either need to be very high so that guests can see around them, or they need to be very low so that guests can see above them. If you have a show or presentation of any sort, steer clear of high centerpieces because they will disrupt your sight lines.
- Are your linens already made? Do you have to pay extra for new ones to be made?
- Do all your vendors provide their own labor, and do they do their own setup and tear-down? Is this an extra cost?

Printed Materials

Your printed materials (save-the-date cards, invitations, RSVP cards, escort cards, place cards, programs, thank-you cards, etc.) are absolutely necessary. Obviously, if you don't have an invitation, how are you to have people attend your party? Some of today's more casual events have "e-vites," but even these events will have a program to hand out to the guests. Printed materials are an event element that actually needs to be considered early on in your event planning. Because of the time it takes to print them, address them, and have them delivered, you'll need to make some printing decisions right away.

Whatever goes out first, whether it's the save-the-date card or the actual invitation, this is your first contact with your guests and their first glimpse of the party. You are conveying to them the type of event they will be attending. Based on the invitation, they will decide what to wear and when to arrive. Do not underestimate the power of the invitation. Have a clear vision of what you want to say because you will be communicating your message with the paper, color, font, ink, language, calligraphy (or no calligraphy), and even the stamp.

At a lot of events, the place-card table is at the entrance. Because it is one of the first impressions of an event, it's a wise investment to make the table stunning. *(John Reilly Photography.)*

When it's time to order your printed materials (we give you a timeline to follow later in this chapter), you'll need to make a few or all of the following design decisions. You'll be choosing a type of card, type of paper, type of printing, ink color, motif, and language. We don't recommend that you choose all your printed materials at the same time. This can be an overwhelming task, and you won't necessarily have all the information you'll need for the program or menu card. But do bring the save-the-date card with you when choosing the invitation, and have the invitation with you when choosing the program and menu card—and bring everything with you when coordinating signage. Showing an example of font and color will produce much better results than describing font and color and ensuring that your "look" is conveyed accurately in your printed materials.

94

There are four basic types of cards. They are single card, bifold card, three-fold card, and booklet. The more information you need to get across, the bigger you'll need to go with your invitation. Most invitations are single or bifold cards. Menus usually are single cards, and programs usually are bifold cards or booklets. Choosing the type of paper for your materials actually can be harder than it seems. There is so much to pick from out there. Hand-pressed paper pulp with flowers or leaves, torn edges, cut edges, heavy cardstock and translucent vellum, patterned, water marked—we can go on and on. Your best bet is to actually touch and hold the paper. Is it heavy enough? Does it feel substantial? Do you prefer something light and layered? Consider the type of party you're planning, and go with the right paper for you. Is it formal? Go with a heavy weight with gilded or torn edges. Is it campy? Go with a fun pattern.

EVENT SUCCESS STORY: GETTING CREATIVE WITH INVITATIONS

Invitation sample from a corporate anniversary party. *(Designed by Scott Redding.)*

We produced a private seventy-fifth birthday party at the Symphony Center, which was the most spectacular party of the year. We originally went to a well-known invitation designer, but the client felt that the original design was way too expensive. The client wanted the design for half the cost, so we had our printer make something similar. We had no idea what was in store for us. It came in multiple pieces that we had to assemble and literally glue together. It took several days and six staff members to put all of the invitations together.

Invitation sample from a groundbreaking ceremony. *(Courtesy of Williams Island).*

Invitation sample from a grand opening. *(Designed by Creative Intelligence.)*

For a corporate anniversary party, we designed an invitation that was a CD using the music of MC Hammer. The entire party was the filming of a music video, and we wanted to set the tone early by getting everyone ready to dance and be part of a team effort. We brought in dancers to choreograph the video, and we broke the guests into groups. Throughout the

(Continued)

95

evening, the guests went from hair and makeup to rehearsals to the green room to the actual filming of the video. At the end of the evening during dinner, the guests got to watch the rough cut of their performance and were swarmed on departure by the paparazzi wanting their autographs and photos. The giveaway was an actual edited version of the music video that was sent to them the day after the event.

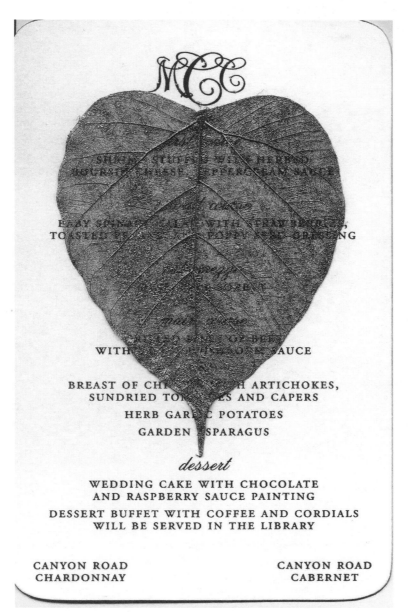

dessert
WEDDING CAKE WITH CHOCOLATE
AND RASPBERRY SAUCE PAINTING

DESSERT BUFFET WITH COFFEE AND CORDIALS
WILL BE SERVED IN THE LIBRARY

CANYON ROAD   CANYON ROAD
CHARDONNAY   CABERNET

Menu card sample from a wedding. *(Designed by Urbane Weddings.)*

If you can get an idea of paper weight and fold, you're ready to check out fonts and ink colors. These decisions can be maddening, but keep your focus simple, and you'll get through it. Fonts break down between serifs (that little curly edge on each letter, such as the print in this book) and sans serifs (like this). A highly stylized, lounge, contemporary event does not call for a super fancy *script*, but if you'd like a script, try one that has a little more *style*, and definitely stay away from an Old English font because that font doesn't exactly convey a modern style. The look and feel of your event should be emulated in the look and feel of your printed materials. If you are planning the company picnic, look for casual invitations with a less fussy font (fussy fonts have lots of curling swirls and are highly embellished). The opposite hold true as well. If your event is high glamour and very elegant, you'll want to check out the fussy fonts that are highly embellished.

A great way to convey a custom look while not spending more is to choose an ink color other than black. As long as you stay with a single-color process, you probably won't pay any more for sienna red than for plain black. Color is a fabulous way to convey the atmosphere of your event. A highly subtle way to communicate the style of your event is through your printing process. The three main ways to print are engraving, embossing, and thermography. Embossing involves placing the wording on plates and pressing the paper on those plates to create a raised look on the sheet. This option, of not using ink, is a little dated and can be hard to read. We stay away from this process unless we're doing something unique with a motif or graphic. Engraving is the most expensive because it is a highly custom process where the paper is pressed with the letters and the ink, creating a raised feel on the paper. Engraving is your best option if you want a completely custom piece. Be aware, however, that it can be *very* expensive, but it is fabulous. If your budget can take it, we say go for it. For the other 99 percent of events out there, thermography is a great alternative. Thermography is a pocess of layering ink on the sheet. To the eye (other than a professional's), you can't tell the difference. The difference is when you feel the printing. Thermography is the least expensive, and if you convey style and elegance with your paper weight, font, and ink color, no one will really ever notice.

While choosing fonts and colors can be exasperating, deciding on language is just plain difficult. There are a million ways to invite someone to a party, but which way is the best way for you? Your best option is to invite someone to a formal event with formal language. The other end of the spectrum holds true as well. But what if your event falls somewhere in between? We suggest getting a little clever with the more common phrases. For example, one couple had a wedding and didn't want to say simply, "Dinner and dancing following ceremony." They wanted to express fun and casual, but not too casual, entertainment. Instead, they said, "Please join us for feasting, libations, and dancing under the stars." They communicated the formal aspect of the wedding through paper weight, ink color, and font but also said hip and fun with their language. You also can make a statement about your event by using a motif or graphic on your printed materials. Don't forget, though, that once you use more than one color, there will be a setup charge and an additional fee for the added color.

When the envelope has professional *calligraphy*, you are speaking volumes about your event. Calligraphy does not necessarily mean black tie, but it does mean style and elegance. Hand calligraphy sets your event apart, and your guests will know that it's something special. You can get a computer to do calligraphy, but there is a difference. Computer calligraphy is a fantastic option if you have 500 or 1,000 envelopes and little to no time. Little to no time in the world of calligraphy is a week or two. A great option for hand calligraphy is custom ink color. A calligrapher can match the ink color on your invitation or make a distinctive complementary color for you. Remember that your address ink color should go with your return address ink color, which probably will be preprinted by your printer.

The final touch of a well-thought-out invitation or save-the-date card is the stamp. It's a small detail, but your guests will notice if you take the time to do it right. When your materials come in, put together a complete invitation (card, vellum, RSVP card, map, etc.), and take the whole thing to the post office. Have the clerk weigh it for you, and then ask to see the choices of stamps. Ideally, you'll find one that works great for your event, works great for your ink color, and is the exact amount you need. If you need 53 cents to send your invitation, but the only exact-amount stamp is of a military tank, it's not your best option for the invitation. Instead, go for two, more attractive 37-cent stamps. In addition, don't forget the RSVP cards; they'll need to be stamped as well. A good tip to keep in mind is to always, always take your invitation to the post office. Don't assume that you know how much it will cost to mail it. Oversized envelopes are more expensive, even if the weight is the same as a regular envelope. Also, ask the post office if they'll hand register the envelopes for you. A lot of envelopes that arrive damaged at your guests' homes are the result of the machine normally used to cancel the stamps. Moreover, you'll want to send one to yourself. In this way, you can get an idea of how long the mail is taking, and you can approximate when you'll begin to get responses. Lastly, if you can help it, don't send anything before any holiday. The mail takes longer, and it's too easy for your invitation to get lost among a bunch of other cards and junk mail.

Your program must coordinate with your other printed materials. Whether you choose color scheme or continue with a graphic or motif, make sure that it all

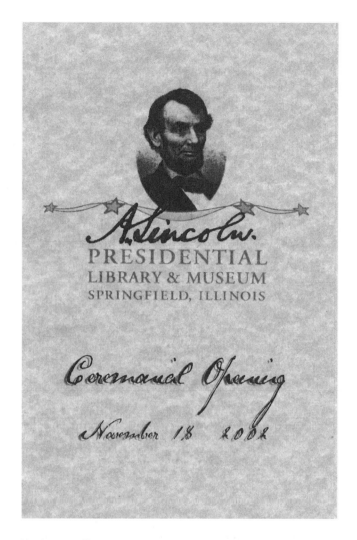

Having a unified look is key to success. All the materials for the Abraham Lincoln Presidential Library Grand Opening (including invitations, credentials, decor, programs, and giveaways) featured the president's signature, as well as the logo and colors of the library. *(Designed by Edelman PR.)*

works together. Most programs include a schedule, list of speakers or hosts, and sometimes even the menu. Programs are very individual, and there aren't any steadfast rules with regard to content. If you want to display the menu card, most put it right at each place setting. For a French service dinner, a menu card is very helpful. Again, don't forget a common thread of color, paper, or motif.

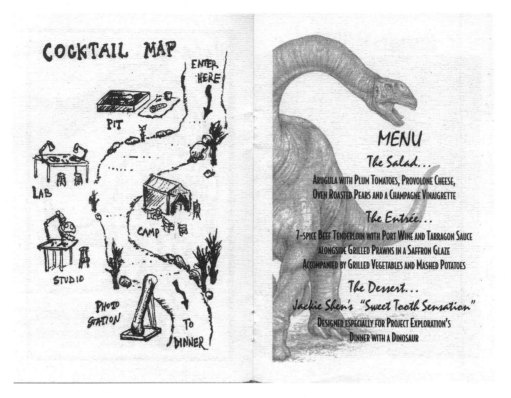

This event's decor included vignettes of a typical dig, so the program, menu, and invitations followed that same look and theme. *(Created by Project Exploration.)*

The last of the most common printed materials is your signage. We think of signage as a way to curb frustration—directional signage, door signage, valet parking signage, registration signage, and sometimes most important, food station signage. With all those scary food allergies out there, displaying cards specifying food items or a *very* knowledgeable waitstaff is essential.

To round out all these materials, there are a few more that you may need. They are

- Table numbers, which can be custom, or if you're in a hotel or using a caterer, they probably have ones for you to use.
- Escort cards, which are usually displayed on a table with a name and table number on each one.
- Place cards, which are at each place setting directing your guests to the exact chair they're supposed to occupy.
- For weddings, there's a host of other printed materials that you can do, such as the engagement announcements, the engagement party invitations,

bridesmaids invitations, rehearsal dinner invitations, and the wedding brunch invitations. If you can host it, there's an invitation for it.

Schedule for Printed Materials

Mapping out your timeline for your printed materials early is essential. If you don't make decisions in a timely fashion, you can be stuck with rush charges or not being able to have exactly what you want. As with everything else in your production timeline, you'll work backwards to determine when you need to make choices. The first step is knowing when certain materials need to be mailed. From there you can add time for choosing the style, printing, and shipping the materials (your invite vendor will give you an exact timeline), and stuffing and addressing (are you doing calligraphy or labels?) the envelopes.

Mailing

Save-the-dates cards	Six months before event
Invitations (mostly out-of-town guests)	Eight or more weeks before event
Invitations (some out-of-town guests)	Six to eight weeks before event
Invitations (mostly in-town guests)	Four to six weeks before event
Rehearsal dinner invitations	Four weeks before event
Wedding brunch invitations	Four weeks before event

Printing and Shipping

Engraving and embossing	Two to four weeks
Thermography	Seven to ten business days
Program	Order to arrive two weeks before event

Calligraphy

Computer calligraphy	Five business days
Custom calligraphy	Two or more weeks (more for high season)
Table numbers, escort cards, place cards, menu card	Five to ten business days

Miscellaneous

Assembly	One or more weeks
Mistake timeline padding	One week

Questions to Ask

- Ask for *real* turnaround times from your printer. How do they ship? Is overnight or rush shipping available? What is the cost for that?
- Ask for *real* turnaround times from your calligrapher. How much for custom colors? Is that a per-envelope charge or a one-time fee or both? Have they done events of this size before? Can you see samples of their work? Which of their font styles do they feel they do the best?
- Ask the post office to hand-verify your invitations.
- Are there any materials that you are printing that can be combined to save money? One example is to have the save-the-date card and hotel information for out-of-town guests printed and/or mailed together.

Tips for Design Success

- Sometimes the decor isn't the most important thing. We can't believe we just wrote that! But it's true. Don't blow your budget on beaded organza linen overlays if they're not right for your event or you know your guests won't get it. If you know your group, you'll know where to draw the line, and that may mean cutting the custom carved ice caviar bar!
- Focus on the most impact for your dollar. If your event is reception style with lots of mingling and less sitting, invest more of your decor dollars in the food stations. Skimp a little on your table centerpieces because most of your guests won't even see them.
- If possible, use atmosphere lighting. Pin-spotting centerpieces and highlighting food stations will give your party pop. No one will ever comment on the magnificently placed lighting cans, but they will talk about your gorgeous flowers or set pieces because they will be able to see them.
- Candlelight! We can't get enough. Use the maximum amount possible because people and things are prettier with candlelight.
- Steer away from "theme-y." Go for atmosphere rather than kitschy. You don't need clowns to say circus. Do it with bold, vibrant linens and bright flowers, and hire a contortionist.
- Your linens *must* go to the floor. Nothing says tacky like exposed metal table legs.
- Size matters. Your decor should be proportionate to your space.

Enhance the Guest Experience

Have you ever seen an Olympic downhill skier right before he slides up to the release chute? Most such skiers are sitting quietly, eyes closed, visualizing the racecourse. They're mentally going through every turn, every ski edge, and every mogul. You must do the same thing for your event, just as if you were attending.

At most events, the guest experience can begin before the guests enter the venue. At this event, the common red carpet entrance was traded for the company color, purple carpet entrance. *(Matthew Kaplan Photography.)*

104

At large public events, a lot of time can be devoted to waiting around. In order to make even waiting-around time entertaining, ski jumpers launched themselves into Baltimore's Inner Harbor. *(Marty Katz.)*

Your guests' experience begins the moment they get in their car or grab a cab and come to your party. And it's not over until they're back in their car or cab. For this reason, you need to picture their evening and forecast their needs from before they even arrive.

Route

Are your guests going to be driving in rush hour traffic? Is there construction on the street where your venue is? If so, your guests may plan to arrive early, which means you need to plan to be ready early. If you're not ready, you can have them greeted with something to eat or something to drink.

Valet

Valet parking and the registration desk *will* make or break your event. These two things are your guests' first experience of the event, and the valet pickup service is their last impression of the event. Everything else can be perfect, but nothing sours a guest like waiting 15 minutes or more for the car. At midnight. In the rain. And their feet hurt.

How your valet runs will be related directly to how many attendants you have. In very general terms, if you have the idea situation, which is a very close parking lot to use or lots of open street parking, and if your guests will be arriving over a length of time, the number of attendants you should have is about one for every 20 expected cars. If the parking lot is a few blocks away and all your guests will be arriving at the same time, you may need as many as one attendant for every five cars. Every situation is different, but being cognizant of your event logistics makes you better prepared. You'll also want to make sure that you have plenty of highly visible signage at valet dropoff, and if your pickup is in a different location, provide directional signage to that location. Is it going to rain? You may want to place greeters with golf umbrellas at valet.

105

Registration

Visible signage at registration is very important. If your registration is in alphabetical order, do not place your letters on the front of the tables. Only your first guests to arrive will see them. The signs should be up high either attached to a post, to a wall, or on an easel above or at eye level. For your V-VIPs, you may want to consider dedicated greeters to help them bypass the regular check-in process.

General Services

These few services are the details that can set your event apart. If there's room in your budget, consider including greeting coat check attendants, bathroom attendants, dedicated greeters, elevator attendants, and dedicated people movers. This extra support will help your event run smoothly and gives it that extra something.

Silent Auction Areas

At most events, the silent auction happens right at the beginning. For this reason, if you're having a silent auction, don't neglect this area when setting it up and decorating it. It should be attractive and work with your other decor, and it also should be efficient. A well-run auction is as important as an interesting auction. This begins with a comprehensive auction log. We've put a sample in Appendix A, but generally, you'll want to maintain a log of the items, where they came from, their bid amounts, and information of that nature. When arranging the auction on site, don't crowd your items, and have lots of people to assist your guests. Put your bid sheets on a clipboard (so that it's easy to write on them) with an attached pen. Then have lots of extra pens as well.

At the close of the auction, you can announce the winner, or if you have many items, you can maintain a winners' board to display after dinner or during dancing.

When you make your bid sheets, they should contain the following:

- Title of item
- Number of item
- Description
- Any restrictions
- Who donated it
- Retail value
- Opening bid
- Bid increments
- Bidder number
- Bidder's table number
- Bid amount

- Final winner
- Any disclaimer

Giveaways

Everybody's heard of the celebrity giveaway bags at the Oscar's or the Emmy's that are filled will electronics, spa vacations, jewelry, and designer clothes. These giveaway bags cost tens of thousands of dollars, but the sentiment of a thank you for your guests is at the heart of those giveaway bags. You can thank your guests for attending as well, but only on a more realistic budget. While giveaways are not required, they are a lovely way to show your appreciation. At the same time, don't compromise the event for the sake of a key chain for each guest.

If you have decided to provide giveaways and are not sure what to give, follow the best gift advice: Make it thoughtful. For example, at a conference we did in the desert, we had monogrammed bags that were filled with desert essentials. They

Custom beach chairs for this beach party served two purposes: (1) seating for the concert and (2) as a giveaway. A giveaway this large worked because all of the guests were local and as such did not need to travel far with the large chair. *(John Reilly Photography.)*

were, among other things, sunscreen, bottled water, a small flashlight to get around the dimly lit hotel property, and a hat. For a recent beach party, we handed out monogrammed canvas lounge chairs that everyone could take home. At a wedding, we boxed up family desserts for the guests' long ride home or to take back to their hotel rooms. Just remember, giveaways are an extra, and while it's great if they're clever, they only need to be thoughtful.

Guests don't always stay until the end of the party. It may seem obvious, but when deciding where and when to put out the giveaways, sometime hosts forget this fact. We like to have the giveaways table set up by the end of dinner. You never know when someone is going to need to leave, but generally everyone stays for dinner. Using the registration table is the handiest, and you have the added bonus of your guests being familiar with that area. If your exit is different from your entrance, you'll want to set up a dedicated area for your giveaways. And with a different exit, you can set up the giveaway table early. We love early when it comes to setup!

Also consider your packaging. It needs to be convenient and attractive—something appealing and easy for your guests. Are most of your guests from out of town? If yes, then reconsider that scale model of the new museum wing as a giveaway. How would they pack that? Out-of-town giveaways are easily packed or used for the trip home.

Questions to Ask

- Does your venue provide any of these services? Most hotels have a coat check area, so you could simply host it. If your venue doesn't have these services in-house, can they source them for you? What would that cost?
- Who is going to distribute your materials? Who will place programs and menu cards and hand out the giveaways?
- Can your venue store your giveaways? Can they put them out for you?
- Can your caterer help with the menu cards? Can your caterer source the labor for coat check?
- Have you arranged for a dedicated phone line in your auction area? If you're accepting credit cards, you'll need the phone line for charge authorizations. Can your venue arrange for the phone line? What would that cost?

Tips for a Positive Guest Experience

- Have a production meeting with all your staff and personnel before the start of the event. A gathering of the minds will ensure that everyone knows their job, as well as important details such as where activities are taking place, where the bathrooms are, and where the stairs or elevator is.

- If possible, have one person in charge of valet, one for registration, and one for giveaways who can each oversee their area. These are easy details to overlook in the heat of the event, and their attention will be valuable.
- When possible, have your valet pickup in a location that is just as convenient as the drop-off location. This may require two different locations if you're guests are moving from one room to another or if your venue is on a one-way street and it's more convenient to move valet for an easier departure. If you do decide to have two locations, don't forget your signage. And don't forget to have your attendant inform your guests as they arrive.
- Good valet service will have an adequate number of attendants, an experienced manager and supervisor, and a thorough plan for communication. Ask for references and if the company has done events at your venue before.
- Look for opportunities for an added touch, such as a coffee and biscotti or Madeline station at the valet pickup so that your guests leave with a warm, sweet memory of your event.
- Check with your city for any upcoming street construction. This may affect your venue decision, your entrance choice, and your valet placement.
- Remember to choose giveaways that are appropriate for the event *and* for your guests.

5

Step Five: Envision Your Event

A great event will appeal to all five of the senses. Your party should look, feel, sound, smell, and taste great. All five senses working together will give you a well-rounded, well-thought-out, and successful party. Menu planning and entertainment selection actually are extensions of the decor phase of event production. Simply put, don't have the Shannon Rovers and serve trifle (a traditional British dessert) at a Mexican fiesta. It just doesn't work. Rather, you would want to consider a Mariachi band and a salsa station. This is an extreme example, but we want to stress the importance of food, beverage, and entertainment at your event. Two elements are essential for a fantastic party: good food and good music. The question is, How should you plan your menu, and how do you choose the right entertainment?

Menu Planning

Food at an event is for all five of your senses. It should look (presentation), smell (yes to garlic and no to smelly fish), feel (firm shrimp, small, bite-sized hors d'oeuvres), sound (made-to-order sizzling croutons), and of course, taste great. Where to begin with menu planning? There's so much to consider.

- What should you serve?
- How should you serve the food?

As discussed later in this chapter, food stations should be abundant with cuisine and creative in presentation because they literally become part of your decor. *(www.jeffellisphoto.com.)*

- When do you serve?
- How much food do you need?
- What should your food presentation look like?
- What kind of bar should you have?
- How much staff do you really need?
- What's fun and different to do?
- Who can help you with all this?

Let's talk about each of these questions.

What Should You Serve?

What you can serve really depends on your budget, your guests, the type of event you're putting together, the type of venue you've chosen, and what your venue or caterer is capable of. As you go through this process of choosing your menu, refer back to your event plan and ask if the cuisine harmonizes with the other elements of your event.

Know your crowd, and know your venue. Choose a menu that is appropriate for the type of group you're hosting. For example, when we do parties that will have a lot of families, we like to have a separate children's menu. Kids generally aren't interested in curry rice and garlic naan, but they always love peanut butter and jelly sandwiches with the crusts cut off or macaroni and cheese and mini-hot dogs. We also like to make the "kiddie station" lower than the regular food stations, making them more kid friendly by making them kid-sized.

Are your guests older, more sophisticated, coming to your event right after work, and is it a networking event? Avoid drippy sauces (they'll be in work clothes), and avoid hors d'oeuvres that are more than one bite because it can be difficult to make conversation between bites or hand out business cards with your hands full.

The type of venue you've chosen also plays a big role in your menu planning. For an outdoor event such as a company picnic, a menu that includes open grills and slowly roasted pork is perfect. If you're venue is a museum, you'll want to consider small hors d'oeuvres (nothing too messy around the art) and a sit-down course.

Ever hear the saying, "Champagne wishes on a beer budget"? When planning your food and beverage, a beer budget really will only get you beer. The best way to approach menu planning is to have a dollar amount in mind. By now you've done a preliminary budget, and you should have an idea of what you have to spend. If you find that you've drastically underestimated your food and beverage costs, ask your venue or caterer to rework the menu (don't short your waitstaff numbers), and at the same time you can massage your budget to get closer to where you want to be. If it's appropriate, you also can consider budget savers such as plasticware rather than china and silver. Also, staffing can be expensive if you do a lot of passing, so maybe you can do self-service stations to help with your labor number.

113

The type of event you're planning will dictate your menu as well. The time of day of your event will influence the kind of food you serve. We just did a high tea at a client's home that took place between 2:00 and 5:00 P.M. outside in July. This event clearly wasn't lunch or dinner, but it still required that we serve something to eat. Considering the warm weather, the outdoor venue, and the fact that it was high tea, we served light hors d'oeuvres and small sandwiches with bite-sized pickup desserts. We knew that the guests would be eating dinner later, so we didn't want to overload them with tons of food, but we also know that at social gatherings, food is a staple. Also, we served champagne, and you never, ever serve alcohol without offering something to eat because your guests need something in their stomachs to keep them from getting inebriated. In addition, warm weather and alcohol on an empty stomach are not a good combination.

If your event is after 5:00 P.M. but ends before 8:00 P.M., you generally can get away with an offering of plentiful hors d'oeuvres (we refer to it as *heavy* hors d'oeuvres). If your event is after 5:00 P.M. but goes late, you'll, of course, serve dinner. If your event is after 9:00 P.M., you may want to consider a dessert reception.

Are you planning a morning conference or meeting? If your conference begins before noon, offer a continental breakfast of cut fruit and pastries with coffee and juices. If your meeting is starts at 11:00 A.M., allot time to serve some lunch, or if it's short and is set to end by 2:00 P.M., offer soft drinks and water with munchies such as cookies or fresh fruits and vegetables. If the meeting is more casual, you can go for something a little out of the ordinary, such as pita chips with an assortment of hummus dips. The extra care you invest in taking care of your guests will not go unnoticed, and it's worth the extra dollars to make them happy and make your event successful.

Don't be concerned about asking your banquet manager or your caterer what he or she recommends for items that are done best. We're lucky to know what caterers in which city do the best plated dinner or the best comfort food or what hotel has the best desserts or the best value for our dollar. You'll need to ask about this up front. You don't want to ask your food and beverage person to serve something that he is not comfortable with.

For example, we did a fall wedding and wanted to serve two French-style signature soups (we'll explain this in the next section), which is how this particular hotel normally served its soups. We didn't really have time for full French service, so we came up with the idea of a soup bar where guests would choose a flavor and have the soups in a coffee mug during the reception hour. After consulting the chef and discussing the logistics of the food station, the venue was very comfortable and very excited about the idea. It ended up being a hit. Now, if the chef weren't on board with our plan, we would have needed to come up with a different plan. Your banquet manager or caterer knows what they're capable of and risking your event's success for an experiment that is beyond the capabilities of your vendor is not worth it.

How Should You Serve the Food?

There are essentially four ways you can do service at your event. You can have waitstaff pass around all the food, you can have food stations offering all the food, you can have your guests seated and have plates served to them at the table, or you can do a combination of all three. There are actually only a few rules to remember when deciding which service to choose.

If you're passing the entire menu, you'll need *a lot* of staff. You want to make sure that each and every guest is approached and offered something to eat. Also, be aware of staff reaching those guests who are farthest away from the kitchen, since a lot of the trays of food can be emptied before they make it to the other end of the room. Most hors d'oeuvres are offered as pieces, and we like to figure a minimum of six pieces per person for a cocktail reception.

If your cocktail hour is short, you may be able to go with fewer pieces per person. If your whole party is reception style, you'll definitely want to offer more pieces per person. When deciding which hors d'oeuvres to pick, you'll want a mixture of types (don't do all seafood such as skewered shrimp, caviar on potato crisps, and smoked salmon on crostini), a mixture of temperatures (do four hot hors d'oeuvres and two cold), and vegetarian options.

If your event is all food stations, the most important factor to consider is to have *plenty* of them. You want to minimize lines by having redundant stations so that your guests can get an item at more than one place. You also want to make sure that your venue/caterer has plenty of staff to replenish the food at the stations. It is very unappetizing to see an almost empty bowl of couscous. You never want to run out of food on a station; rather, you want the items to be replenished before they're emptied so that the station always looks fresh and full.

An option for food stations is to have chefs at the stations carving, sautéing, or mixing to give a liveliness to the event. Or you could have waitstaff serving the food. This will be more expensive, so if it's not in your budget, you also can have the food on the station, and the guests can serve themselves.

When doing a full sit-down meal, there are basically two options of service. The first, which is what most people are accustomed to, is English service. This is where waiters arrive at each table with the plated course and place it for each guest. Certain variations can happen, such as a preset salad course.

The second way to do a sit-down meal is to do French service. This is where waiters (and you'll need lots of staff for this style) approach each guest with platters of courses, serving them individually. To use the soup example from earlier, French service would mean two or more waiters each would have a different bowl of soup and then ask each guest which they would prefer, and then the waiter would ladle the fresh soup into the soup bowl, which had been placed already. Each course, even the coffee course, is offered in this way. This is very elegant and upscale and also requires a lot of time and a healthy budget. French style also requires a venue and a caterer with a lot of experience in this type of service. It's fabulous, and for all of these reasons, it's also rare.

Our favorite way to serve food is a combination of all of these. We like to pass hors d'oeuvres and have food stations at receptions. Passing food and some drinks

115

EVENT SUCCESS STORY: RULES CAN BE BROKEN!

Continuity is key to menu planning, as well as to the presentation of food. A beautiful presentation of hors d'oeuvres, food stations, and a plated dinner set the stage for the party. People eat with their eyes as well as their mouths. The most important thing to remember is you must have a tasting before the event, which will allow you to see the presentation style as well as sample the dishes from your proposed menu.

Many venues tell you that they have an exclusive caterer and that nothing can be brought in, but rules are made to be broken. If you are unhappy with anything during the tasting, you are entitled to speak your mind and demand whatever corrections necessary to make your event perfect.

When planning a menu for a New York wedding at a venerable private club, we ran into a few challenges with the menu planning. First, the club had its own kitchen, and it wasn't very flexible. And when it came to the tasting, we were so disappointed that we knew that the only way to fix this for the client was to convince the club to waive its house rules. We convinced the club to allow us to bring in many items to enhance the receptions both before and after the dinner by requesting items that it was not able to provide. By combin-

Custom minicakes were each a work of art. *(John Reilly Photography.)*

ing the club's entrée and the food we brought in for the reception and desserts, we created a menu that wedded a glorious presentation and outstanding flavors. We brought in Nobu to offer its sushi and smoked salmon. We brought in Grace's Market to provide the passed hors d'oeuvres. The only thing we asked the club to do was the soup and the entrée. Immediately following the toasts, guests were invited downstairs for desserts and dancing. We surprised them with a full dessert display that featured 60 special mini-wedding cakes displayed by famous cake designer Sylvia Weinstock. We also offered assorted individual soufflés, poached pears made to order and drizzled with hot fudge, Bananas Foster, and a selection of pickup sweets. Each cake was whimsically decorated and incredibly elaborate. Ornamentations included fresh flowers, sugar paste blossoms, marzipan fruits, and piped swirls of frosting, ribbon, and lacework. Each one was a different color, motif, shape, and style. This dessert station was definitely one of the highlights of the evening.

We encountered this same resistance when planning a private party at a club in Los Angeles, where we decided to select food items that the caterer could not make in-house. This allowed us to bring in Peking duck from Mr. Chow's, sushi from Matsuhisa, green corn tamales from El Cholo, and cakes from Hansen's. When you are able to provide a wide variety of food from the very best places, the guests do notice, and it always makes for a more successful event.

Floral trees act as the final touches to the sushi station. *(Richard Shay Photography.)*

alleviates the lines at the food stations. And food stations alleviate the anxiety of everyone having access to something to eat. After the reception, doing two or three courses where your guests sit is ideal, especially if you have a performance, speeches, or a program. Then it's always great to get your guests up again for after-dinner drinks or coffee and a few passed sweets such as biscotti (which goes well with coffee) or chocolate-covered strawberries.

When Should You Serve?

Always, always, always offer your guests something to drink right away, even if it's just sparkling waters. If you do offer wine or you have a bar open from the beginning, you want to give your guests something to eat with it. As we've mentioned, avoid serving liquor to guests with empty stomachs. We talked about the timing of food service in Chapter 2, but when should you have courses bused? During a reception, you'll want busing staff to be out in your space at all times, helping to keep your party good looking and fresh. If you have a sit-down dinner with speeches and a program, you'll want to discuss timing with your venue/caterer. Busing should occur between speeches or before your program. This goes for coffee service as well. Coffee service generally is the noisiest to serve.

How Much Food Do You Need?

As you work with your venue/caterer, remember that you'll need to give them a guaranteed guest count approximately three business days before your event date. This allows them ample time to order the food and supplies they'll need for your party. After those 72 hours, you can increase your guest count (not by a hundred, but certainly by 10 or 20 people), but you cannot decrease your guest count. The venue/caterer has already purchased foodstuffs for your guaranteed amount, and they won't be allowed to return anything to account for a lower guest count.

What happens if you have four extra people show up the day of the event? Don't worry; your venue/caterer has prepared food for approximately 5 percent over the guest guarantee. Therefore, as long as you have room, they'll be prepared with enough food. Certain menu items always seem to be extra popular at events, and in turn, we always order extra of these items in the hope of not running out of them. Generally, you can't overorder shrimp cocktail or sushi (the more common rolls, such as California, avocado, and spicy tuna). Whether these items are passed or placed on a food station, people *love* to eat shrimp cocktail and sushi at parties.

A decadent display of whole lobsters can be quite the budget buster, but if you have the funds for a presentation such as this, it can leave a lasting impression on your guests. *(PWEE Staff.)*

Order extra. Then there's items that are not as popular but are nice to have, for example, a raw bar that has caviar and vodka. It's a great showpiece, but it's definitely not for everyone. You won't need to order enough caviar for every guest; you can underorder an item like this.

What Should Your Food Presentation Look Like?

119 ▶

Oddly enough, your food stations should be overflowing and full, and your plated courses should be neat, appealing, and not filled to the edges of the dish. As each guest approaches a food station, it should be abundant with food and look like that guest is the first one to get there. Sparsely filled platters and bowls are not appetizing and look as if they've been picked over. Also, if you can avoid chafing dishes, your food station will be more decorative and less cafeteria looking. Consult with your venue/caterer on how they plan to set up the food stations and also how they normally replenish dishes as an event is in progress. If they know that you're aware of the food presentation, they will be too.

The perfect plated presentation is a coordinated effort between you, the client, and the chef. Working together to create a beautiful plated course will take at least one tasting and, on site, a team of professionals behind the scenes. *(PWEE Staff.)*

A plated course should be presented like artwork. It should be attractive and colorful. (Avoid white fish with mashed potatoes. Instead, consider a colorful starch such as butternut squash or sweet potato.) Also limit the number of sauces. If your meat is served with a sauce, don't plate side dishes with sauces as well. They'll mix, and then who knows what flavors you're making on a single plate of food. If your venue/caterer suggests lots of sauces for each food item, we would question the quality of the meat or vegetables. When doing large events, sauces often are used to cover a dry piece of meat or a tasteless vegetable. Beware.

Placing your food stations and tables is also an important part of food presentation. When working with your space, you will want to have your food stations located in accessible areas not just for your guests but also for your kitchen staff. They'll need to be spaced throughout the venue in such a way that they are easily spotted and easily replenished. Don't put them in tight corners or too close to entrances, where you can create a bottleneck of bodies. Don't put them too close to stages or too close to tables where your guests will be sitting. Food stations need lots of room and are best on the walls of the event. Tables for sit-down meals need to have about five or six feet between them. You must account for chairs to be pulled all the way out from the table (two feet) and space to walk between the chairs (another two feet). As with food stations, you want to allow ample space at entrances and kitchen access areas. Try not to put guest tables close to speakers (or make sure that you have a younger group at the tables that are close to speakers).

What Kind of Bar Should You Have?

The type of bar you use really depends on your budget. There are a lot of options to make a bar cost-effective without making it a cash bar (which is our least favorite option and generally frowned on). A fully hosted bar can either be paid on a consumption basis, or you can buy a bar package. When paying on consumption, you are charged a certain amount per drink, with prices varying for bottled water, soft drinks, beer, wine, and mixed cocktails. If your group is not a heavy drinking group, such as a group with a lot of families or an older crowd, buying the bar on a consumption basis is a smart choice. If your group has a lot of partiers, and you know they'll drink a lot of mixed cocktails, you may want to consider a bar package.

There are two things that are nice about bar packages. First, with a group that drinks a lot, you actually may pay less. Second, you know up-front what you're going to pay because the package is based on a per-person, per-hour rate. It won't change (unless you have overtime), and no surprises with your budget can be very good.

Another decision you have to make is what kind of bar you want to provide. You can have a premium bar, which would include top-shelf liquors such as Ketel One vodka. You can have a standard bar, which would include less expensive liquors such as Smirnoff vodka. Or you could choose to have a bar that just offers beer, wine, and soft drinks. Obviously, the premium bar is the most expensive option, but as we mentioned before, if you know your group well, you'll know which of these bar options will work best for your event and for your budget. We have found over the years that our clients always want the premium bar with top-shelf liquor, and they also want liqueurs (such as Bailey's or Kahlua) offered as well.

In addition to the bars, you also may like to have your waitstaff offer wine at the guest tables. This is an added expense, so you'll want to confirm with your venue/caterer the per-bottle charge for a service such as this. Keep in mind that your venue/caterer will tell you how many bottles of white wine, how many bottles of red wine, and if you choose, how many bottles of champagne you'll need.

When calculating how many bottles you'll need, your venue/caterer will rely on some industry standards. For example, a regular bottle of white wine will render approximately six glasses per bottle. Since white wine should be chilled, the glass should never be filled to the top, or your wine will lose its chill (especially on a warm day at an outdoor event). A bottle of red wine or champagne will render approximately five to six glasses per bottle. Ask your contact person how the staff pours; also ask if you'll be charged for unopened bottles. If you're providing the wine or champagne, make sure that the servers know that you plan to return all unopened, unchilled bottles and cases for a refund. In this way, they will be careful to open and chill the bottles as they need them.

How Much Staff Do You Really Need?

A good staff that provides you with excellent service is *just as important* as the food itself. A good staff will keep your site clean with proficient busing, your food stations full with replenished food, and your guests happy with quick, knowledgeable service. You cannot overestimate the importance of experienced waitstaff.

Because of these things, the staff is the last place to skimp on your food and beverage. When you're planning the menu with your venue/caterer, discuss the staffing plan. How many busers do they have? Do they have dedicated people to staff and replenish the food stations? How many waitstaff per table do they plan to have? The staff count is based on a few things. First, what your menu calls for. If you have a sushi station where a chef is preparing rolls, that requires extra staff. If you have a chef carving tenderloin or preparing omelets to order, that will also be extra.

Another factor in staffing numbers is where the kitchen is located. If you're at a site where the kitchen is far from the main event area or on a different floor, you'll definitely need additional staff. There are some industry standards that you can use as guidelines. Generally, you can figure one bartender per 100 guests. We prefer one bartender per 75 guests (we hate lines at the bars and food stations), especially if it's a premium bar where your bartender is mixing and pouring drinks, but you often can get away with one per 100 people. If your bar is strictly beer, wine, and soft drinks, where your bartender is simply pouring drinks, you probably can do with one bartender per 120 guests. Again, depending on the type of bar and the type of crowd, you many want to add or subtract some bartending staff.

At a sit-down meal with English service, you'll want about two waiters per table. If you're doing French service, you'll need double that number. The key to a sit-down course is to have all your guests at the table served at the same time. If your event is reception style, where you'll be passing hors d'oeuvres, you'll want one waiter per 15 guests passing. If you have a large event (100 or more guests), you'll want about one waiter per 20 (maybe even 25) guests passing. Ask your venue/caterer what they normally provide.

What's Fun and Different to Do?

There's almost no limit to what you can do for a party. We've done everything from suspend a food station from the ceiling, to having a model wear a costume that acts as a lazy Susan to offer hors d'oeuvres, to simply having food items freshly made at the station. The most fun things to do are specialty interactive bars. These are stations such as a mashed potato bar, a hot fudge sundae bar, or a risotto bar. Food stations where your guests can pick and choose toppings are always fun.

We like coming up with new types to do something different. Ask your venue/caterer for suggestions. Specialty food stations where something unusual is made right in front of your guests is something fun to do as well. Our latest favorite is tortilla and guacamole stations. The aroma and action of watching food prepared is a good conversation maker.

At theme parties, we like to dress up the waitstaff. For example, at a rock and roll party we had a number of the waitstaff passing mini-cheeseburgers while on roller skates and dressed as car hops. For something different at your party, consider having your favorite restaurant come in to do a specialty dish (make sure that it's okay with your venue). At an event we did in New York, we had a popular sushi restaurant, Nobu, come in to do the sushi station. They brought in sushi rolls that were already prepared and then did hand rolls and pieces at the party. Guests were thrilled to have such a popular restaurant right at their private party.

You don't always have to go high end either. For one of our clients whose favorite cheeseburger is from In-N-Out in California, we knew the fast-food restaurant had a kitchen trailer that they take to special events. Offering In-N-Out's famous Double Double's was a huge and different hit of the party. All you need to do is get creative and then get approval.

Who Can Help You with All of This?

Your primary help will come from your banquet captain (such as at a hotel) or your caterer. Beyond that, you may get to meet the chef or sous chef, who also will be able to help you with menu ideas or variations on the standard menu. Your venue and/or caterer, if they're experienced and good at what they do, will have or will be able to get any answers you many need with regard to your food and beverage menu. As long as you're well informed about your event and your guests, and as long as you ask good questions, either of these people will make excellent guides to this process.

Questions to Ask

- Ask your caterer if he or she has worked in your venue before. Does he or she have experience with the kitchen available? How has he or she handled challenges in the past? What would he or she recommend to help make your event a success?
- Has your venue done a similar event to yours before? How did it work? What should you or shouldn't you do differently?
- What are your venue's/caterer's signature dishes? What do they feel they do best? Can they provide the kind of service you're looking for? Can you meet your banquet captain?
- Is the gratuity taxable in your state? It's different from state to state, and if the gratuity is taxable, it will increase your budget.
- Are gratuities given to your captains, or do you need to tip separately?

Tips for Menu Success

- When choosing hors d'oeuvres, pick a mixture of hot and cold items.
- Pay attention to the content; you don't want to be repetitive. If you're serving lobster as a main course, don't do a lobster hors d'oeuvre.

- Include plenty of vegetarian options in your entire menu. If you have a sit-down dinner where everyone is getting the same thing, make sure that you ask what the vegetarian option is.
- Make sure that your venue/caterer can provide kosher meals. If not, you may need to order those separately.
- Ask that your staff be well informed. All staff that is going to be around your guests (food station chefs and servers) should know all the contents of the menu. When it comes to allergies, the best defense is for the staff to know the ingredients of all the menu items. There are so many allergies out there that you can't possibly accommodate them all without compromising the menu. Your servers and busers also should know where the closest restroom is.
- When we do for large groups of people, we may offer alternate meals for vegetarians or for people on kosher diets.
- When you do your food and beverage, don't forget to include your staff and any production crew and talent. We'll cover crew and talent hospitality in Chapter 6.
- Order extra of the known popular items (shrimp cocktail) and light on the less popular items (caviar). Your venue/caterer will help you to determine which items fit in which category.
- Remember to be creative and get approval from your venue or caterer for any unusual plans.

Entertainment

All clients ask us what kind of entertainment they should have at their event. As with the rest of this event-production process, choosing the entertainment it only the first step. After you figure out what the right entertainment is, you then have to find it, and then you need to produce the entertainment.

Essentially, entertainment comes in four forms: incidental, interactive, live bands, and name talent. Incidental entertainment is like filler acts. They won't be featured acts, but they round out the event. Some examples are close-up magicians, dancers, artisans, and marching bands. Interactive entertainment is also used as filler acts, but your guests usually come away with something. Game shows, tarot card readers, and creation stations are good examples of interactive entertainment and activities. The most popular form of entertainment is live bands; dance bands, trios, background music, choirs, and mariachis are some of the most common types

EVENT SUCCESS STORY:
WHEN IT COMES TO ENTERTAINMENT, KNOW YOUR AUDIENCE

Entertainment can make or break your event. When the entertainment is great, the party is great. If the entertainment isn't perfect or doesn't fit the crowd, it can have a negative effect on the rest of the evening. Certain events are more suited for name talent than others. If your evening is message-driven or has a very skewed audience, then you shouldn't have a comic. You never know if someone is going to be offended by the jokes.

We have been in a few situations where the client insisted on a certain performer because the CEO loved the comic or someone saw a recent HBO special and thought it was hysterical. We always try to talk the client out of this situation, but ultimately, we have to give the client what he wants, and sometimes the comic just isn't funny. We have had comics bang on their microphone and say, "Can you hear me out there?" This is when you know they are fighting to find the crowd and get them back into their show. Some comics don't have enough material to perform for more than 20 minutes, and there are a very select few who can perform for more than 60 minutes. The key is to see the act live before you book it for an event.

You also always need to know your audience. When we produced all 250 live performances in the athlete village at the 1996 Summer Olympics, the key factor in choosing entertainment was to have musical acts that transcended language for a diverse audience of athletes, coaches, and officials from all over the world, with ages that ranged from the teens to the 60s. There was something special about watching the world unite over music during the games; athletes from all over the world came together to dance in the club, chill out in the coffee house, or cheer for Arnold Schwarzenegger as he received the key to the Olympic Village.

Arnold Schwarzenegger receives the key to the Athlete Village at the 1996 Summer Games. *(PWEE Staff.)*

Knowing your guests will be the single most important factor in choosing the right entertainment. Determine the type of crowd you have by the average age, gender, and whether they're attending as couples, singles, or families. For example, at a corporate dinner where there will be primarily older businessmen coming directly from work without spouses or dates, you will want to avoid a dance band. Most likely business colleagues and networking don't make for the right dancing atmosphere. Rather, you'll want to provide ambient music to create a relaxed mood and provide some entertainment to jump-start conversations. Try background music such as a jazz group, and add some unusual incidental entertainment such as an authentic Asian candy sculptor or a performance piece. This is really basic, but it'll work.

If your audience is mostly families, you'll want to have plenty of entertainment that appeals to kids. Try creation stations, miniparades, and a fun band. Interactive entertainment is good for all ages. As long as it's appropriate for your party, try activities that engage your guests.

The talent at your event will dictate the mood of your event. We like to create events that build to either a fantastic crescendo (such as a fireworks display or a big show) or a big crescendo that then winds down at the end, where late-night guests can reflect on the evening and chat (such as having a late-night menu that includes waffles at 2:00 A.M. and a pianist).

What kind of mood are you trying to construct? Are your guests flowing in and out of the event? You'll need short bursts of excitement, so you'll want bright performances, say, every hour or 90 minutes. You could try a performance group (such as dancers) or authentic ethnic groups (such as a Chilean band or a salsa band) that are unusual and visual as well as interesting to talk about. Consider your flow, and then work in where you need music, performance, activity, or shows.

Finding Entertainment

Sometimes you know what kind of feeling you want to create, but you don't know exactly how to create it. This is where finding the entertainment can be helpful. We're lucking because a lot of the time the acts find us. Every day our mail is full of CDs, videos, or DVDs of one act or another. Some of them are innovative and great, and some aren't so great. There are times when our library of talent is missing that perfect fit for that certain event.

In such situations, we have three main avenues to find that special act for our events. The first and most helpful is the Internet. It's amazing what you can type into a search engine and the amount of qualified information you get back! An-

EVENT SUCCESS STORY:
KNOW WHAT WILL ATTRACT ATTENDEES

We produce many mall grand openings, and the most important part of the celebration (and the ultimate goal of the developer) is the guest experience. We work closely with the client to effectively align the grand opening with the surrounding community and the client's marketing plan and attempt to attract a new customer demographic as well.

A fashion show creates a happening for the crowds while also involving retailers in a shopping mall grand opening. *(Courtesy of Urban Retail Group.)*

A great example of this is the grand opening of the Citrus Park Town Center in Tampa, Florida. We started the two-week grand opening festivities with a building reveal (ribbon cutting), a balloon release that sent 8,000 balloons into the sky, a pyro blast, a marching band, cirque-like characters, and tons of incidental entertainment throughout the mall. That same day we had a free public concert featuring KC & The Sunshine Band, Disco Inferno, and a 20-minute fireworks display.

A free, open to the public concert and fireworks display not only punctuated the grand opening festivities but also provided a medium for the developer to thank the community. *(PWEE Staff.)*

Through the ensuing days, we produced many forms of entertainment, talent, and features. One of the most successful was the fashion show using the shopping center retailers and featuring the season's latest trends and fashion offerings. We featured a collection of the designer merchants as the professional models mixed with fully choreographed dancers that made their way down the custom runway. The different segments featured music, lighting, choreography, and special effects throughout the opening weekend.

The "talk of the town" was the game show. The Hollywood-style game show had dazzling lights, bells, buzzers, buttons, and a spinning wheel. Everyone had a chance to win prizes such as gift certificates to the Citrus Park stores and restaurants, theater tickets, and a grand prize shopping spree. The master of ceremonies brought up contestants from the audience, and this generated hours of crowd involvement.

Another type of feature to draw crowds was autograph sessions with various athletes. To round out the program, we brought in numerous incidental entertainers, as well as children's entertainment and a music series.

other helpful avenue is to contact incidental entertainment agencies. If you go on the Internet and find one act that is close to what you're looking for, that act usually is represented by an agency. The agency has a whole host of other acts it represents. You can get some really good ideas that you may not have thought of.

Another opportunity is to just keep your eyes open. In every major city there are street performers. In fact, about 15 years ago we booked three men who sang a cappella at a train station. Today their music is played on the radio across the country, and they have five albums out! What's also great about street performers is their authenticity. Every kind of ethnic group can be found on the most populated street corners. Peruvian groups, drum groups, living statues, Chilean flute musicians, and Mariachi bands are a short list of acts we've booked just from walking past them on the street.

Name Talent

If the band's together or the comedian hasn't retired, by and large you can have anyone at your private event. It'll cost you, but it can be done. What's different about

As part of Harley Davidson's centennial celebration, the client spared no expense and opted for BB King to perform at the Harley Owner's Group event. *(PWEE Staff.)*

name talent is that the world of celebrity and name entertainment has its own set of rules, language, and procedures. Never, never, never try to negotiate, book, and produce a name act on your own. Other than it's a complicated process not left to the inexperienced, most likely if you're able to find the representing agent, he or she may not take your call! If you would like to book a name act for your event, you are going to need a professional who is experienced not just in producing events but also in producing entertainment.

When it comes to hiring name talent, there are some basics that are good to know. First, name acts charge more for private events than for their ticket show. A performance fee for name talent runs the range from a few thousand dollars to millions of dollars. Second, even if your budget can accommodate the performance fee, they still may not take the date. Third, if they take the date, their fee is just the beginning. You'll need to cover their expenses (that includes getting them to the city of your event, putting them up in a hotel of their choice, providing transportation for them, and even feeding them). Fourth, name acts don't come alone. They have managers, crew, stylists, costumers, assistants, makeup artists, and friends. You are responsible for all these people for the duration of your act's stay in whatever city your event takes place.

133

Jay Leno flew in just for this performance at the Michael Jordan Foundation benefit gala. While this was generous on his part, it took a lot of juggling to get him to Chicago after he taped his Friday show and back in plenty of time to begin working on his Monday show. *(Courtesy of Michael Jordan Foundation.)*

The fifth basic to name entertainment is production. The large fee you're paying the artist does not cover the production costs. Production is part of any act you book. This includes anything from a jazz trio to a jazz legend. Production is sound, staging, lighting, and labor. We also consider production to include hospitality. While small local acts don't always require that you feed them, we make it a policy to take care of our performers at our events. With name talent, you will be required to not just feed the crew and band but also to feed them what they ask for. Everybody's heard about the horror stories of bands asking for cases of beer or Simpson's videos or fish on Tuesdays. Well, they're not just stories. Name acts ask for a ton of stuff in their contract, and food is just the beginning. You'll need to provide them with ground transportation, hotel accommodations, and sometimes per diems. There are many unforeseen costs associated with name talent, and for this reason alone, we strongly recommend that you hire a professional to help navigate you through the process.

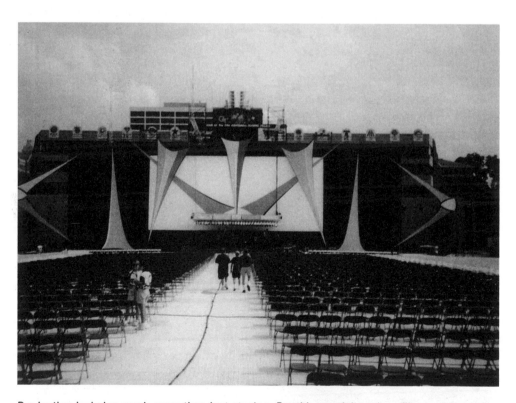

Production includes much more than just staging. For this special outdoor film premier during the 1996 Summer Olympics, it also included a 100-foot screen, stretch fabric for a reveal, plastic covering for the football field, and approximately 10,000 chairs. *(PWEE Staff.)*

Production for all other kinds of entertainment is significantly simpler. First on your checklist should be sound and lighting requirements. Does the band bring its own lighting? Do you need to provide it? What does the band require? Most local bands will bring their own sound, so you'll just need to provide them with power for their equipment. If this is the case, you need to ask the band what their power requirements are and then forward those needs to your venue. Lighting can be optional and at your discretion. You'll want to decide if spending the money on special lighting for the band is essential or right for your event. If it is, you can source it through your venue or ask your band to bring lighting with them that you can pay for. Ideally, you'll have a sound company to coordinate all these logistics for you. Not every event warrants hiring a sound and lighting company, but if you have a lot of acts or a large event, it would be beneficial to work with one.

Next on your checklist is staging. Maybe your event won't need it, but bands always look better and show better at an event when they're raised up on a stage. If you're at a hotel, the hotel probably has its own platform staging in-house and can

This rotating stage allowed all the guests to see the entertainment perform throughout the evening. *(PWEE Staff.)*

set that up for you. Last are labor requirements. Entertainment production always has a labor line item in the budget. If you have a sound and lighting vendor, he will coordinate the labor needed for the production at your event. If your venue is providing you with sound and lighting, he also will contract any labor you'll need.

Every party needs entertainment. But don't think that you need to blow your whole budget on live music or name talent. Your event may only need some recorded music, a DJ, or simply a pianist. Other events are driven by the entertainment and need layers of different kinds of music, performance acts, and interactive talent. Don't be discouraged by the abundance of choices, and don't spend time wondering what you should do. Go with your instincts on how much entertainment is right for your party, and then go ahead and do your research. Watch videos or DVDs on possible acts, go see them perform at another event, and listen to their tapes or CDs. When you come across the right one, you'll know it, and it'll be the perfect fit!

Questions to Ask

- What are your act's technical requirements?
- Is your act available for overtime? If so, how much is the overtime?
- How does your act perform? When do they take breaks? How long are their breaks? Can they perform continuously without breaks?
- Is there space in your venue to stage your acts before they perform and where they can change and rest while they're not performing?
- Do they need to do a sound check? How long is their sound check? Remember that almost every act should need a sound check. Even speakers or DJs need to come early to see where they will be, rehearse, and do a sound check.

136

Tips for Talent Success

- Go authentic. Ethnic groups are more interesting not just for their sound but also for their dress.
- Get a CD, DVD, or video. If you've never worked with a particular act before, you'll want to check them out first. If they don't have any of these, ask if you can go see them perform somewhere.
- What is the band's attire? If it's not some authentic ethnic group you'll want the talent to be dressed according to the event attire.
- Don't be afraid of using wildly different kinds of music at one event.

Next Steps

- You've found your band, you've booked your band, and now you're ready to finalize (or as much as you can finalize) your event timeline.
- Work in your band performance times, when you're going to open the food stations or bars, when you're going to seat for dinner, and when dancing will begin.
- Also, don't forget to include the event end time.

All these details will be important as we move on to the next step of successful event planning.

6

Step Six:
Finish with the Unseen Details

Unseen details, or the back stage of your event, are the glue of your event. Nothing happens, or happens smoothly, without a highly organized operations plan, a competent staff, and a thorough security plan.

These three areas—operations, staffing and volunteers, and security—are where you make event production look so easy and how you're going to make your colleagues and friends think you're a pro. Some of the best, most creative plans never come to fruition because of a poor operations plan, inadequate staffing, or something that happened with security. In this chapter you'll learn the ins and outs of these three key unseen details, and you'll learn how you, too, can make it look so easy.

Operations

An event either does or does not go smoothly depending on how well you've managed your operations. Coordinating the efforts of all your vendors with the venue, with your staff, and with your client (if there's one involved) is what makes up an operations plan—when they arrive, where they arrive, how they load in, where they set up, how they manage their piece of the puzzle, and finally, how they tear down and load out. You will need to oversee all these pieces and make sure that they work together seamlessly.

EVENT SUCCESS STORY: TIMING IS EVERYTHING

Part of our production of the grand opening ceremony of the Abraham Lincoln Presidential Library and Museum consisted of two giant, inflatable video screens. The screens would be used to IMAG the stage ceremony as well to show an address by President George W. Bush and a specially produced Gettysburg Address video.

We arranged for street plans from the city to ensure that the two screens would span the width of the two streets that bordered the front of the library. What we would later find out the night before the event was that the plans that we were given represented the street layout prior to completion of the library. Part of the construction process called for the building to extend past the sidewalks, pushing them further out and thus narrowing the street, and narrowing our precise screen measurements. When we put the screens up, they extended over the curb and onto the sidewalk. Fortunately, the fact that the screens were inflatable made them soft enough on the bottom that they formed around the curb.

An element of the opening sequence was a flyover by the local Air National Guard. Although usually limiting flyovers to aviation-related events and high-profile sporting events, the guard made an exception, given the political nature and the historic importance of the event. The plan was to have four F-16's fly over just at the conclusion of the National Anthem. We sent an event timeline to the commanding officer, who was able to coordinate a training flight to coincide with the event.

President George W. Bush addresses the crowd at the Abraham Lincoln Presidential Library and Museum dedication. *(John Reilly Photography.)*

About 20 minutes before the scheduled flyover, a pilot from the unit arrived to our site with a hand-held radio to communicate with the pilots in the air. Apparently it is more difficult to contact four F-16s traveling at 400 miles per hour with a small hand-held radio than the pilots realized. By the time the pilot on the ground was able to contact the four jets in the air, they were only ten seconds out! Fortunately, Miss America had just begun the last verse of her rendition of the National Anthem, and the jets roared overhead as she finished—just as we planned.

EVENT SUCCESS STORY:
CHOREOGRAPHING MULTIPLE VENDORS WITH EASE

Since 1995, we have managed the corporate hospitality village at the Air and Sea Show in Ft. Lauderdale, Florida. The event is billed as the largest two-day spectator event in the world because it annually draws over four million people. It is unquestionably one of the most labor-intensive and operationally complex events that we produce, and it takes almost the entire staff out of the office for eight days.

Our involvement is not limited to corporate hospitality, although that is our primary focus. Additionally, we assist in the setup of the mile-long display village, an area for sponsors and vendors to distribute and sell their materials. We also manage a VIP event for sponsors, performers, and high-ranking military officers on the Friday night before the show begins. Finally, we produce a free public concert for about 50,000, followed by night flybys of military jets and a fireworks show choreographed to music. Needless to say, it is quite an undertaking, but it has become increasingly seamless over the years.

B1 bombers fly over the crowd of nearly 4 million people. *(Courtesy of MDM Group.)*

The operations begin the Monday prior to the show, which always happens the first weekend in May. At 5:00 A.M., the city closes down Route A1A, the major intercoastal highway, for approximately three miles. At this point we begin marking the street using a measuring tape, electrical tape, and permanent markers. These markings indicate the exact placement of every tent, trailer, restroom, truck, ice bin, and any other piece of equipment that will be housed within the operations area over the coming week. Everything from the five feet of walk space between the bathroom trailer and the fencing truck to the 340 feet of south-end hospitality tents is accounted for. The marking process alone once took over four hours because it covers nearly a three-mile-long stretch of highway, but through greater fluency with both the event site and the map that is used as the guide, the process now takes closer to two hours. While this process is taking place, the fencing company encloses the entire hospitality

(Continued)

area with a temporary six-foot fence. The enclosed area takes up approximately four lanes of traffic and leaves the other two as pedestrian and fire lanes.

Over the ensuing five days, numerous vendors load into the operations area. These vendors range from the tent company, to the soft drink and water suppliers, to the balloon provider, whose 25-foot balloon, which is set up on the beach, serves as the show center indicator for the pilots performing in the show. The first and arguably the most operationally important delivery is the operations trailer. The trailer is set up as an on-site command center, complete with Internet, phone and fax lines, maps of all air show-related sites, and a separate office that houses the fire and police representatives on show days. Someone from our staff is stationed in the trailer at all times while we're on site. The deliveries continue throughout the week at a regimented pace. This schedule has been refined annually over our time of producing the event and represents another one of the advantages of doing the same event from year to year.

Over time, we have come to learn which vendors can load in at the same time without interfering with each other or clogging up the limited access routes within the operations area. Without this consideration, these routes easily can become congested with trucks, forklifts, and golf carts. The staff golf carts, another by-product of experience, have become one of the allowances that enable the staff to survive the week of repeatedly trekking back and forth throughout and beyond the operations area (about a three-mile stretch) in the Florida sun, heat, and humidity.

As the week progresses, our staff splits into groups. One team continues placing vendors within the operations area, while another team assists with load-in of the display village, which is located just beyond the south end of the operations area on the street that sees the majority foot traffic. This group greets the vendors, explains parking and arrival times, and

142

Pool decor at the VIP party. *(Steve Kirsh.)*

takes them to their tent locations—another instance where the golf carts are useful because some of the locations are over two miles away. Yet another team begins the setup and execution of the Friday night VIP event at a local hotel ballroom and pool.

Everyone for the most part handles the same responsibilities from year to year while at the same time being familiar enough with the other duties to step in when needed.

The five days of load-in and setup build up to the actual show days, Saturday and Sunday. Saturday is easily the longest day of the week. We arrive on site at 5:00 A.M. to make sure that all the hospitality tents are completely set, and to oversee that catering has breakfast prepared for the guests, who typically arrive well before we open the gates at 9:00 A.M. Everyone has a group of tents that they are responsible for managing over the two show days. Over the course of the day, we continue to supervise catering to ensure that food is replenished and changed from breakfast to lunch and lunch to snacks when it is supposed to be. Additionally, we oversee the security and volunteers who staff the only two entrances to the hospitality area, one at the north end and one at the south end, as well as the security that are stationed at each individual tent to ensure that the guests are in the areas where they belong in. On top of this, there is a constant string of various medical situations (most of which are related to the heat), lost children, and even more lost parents that need to be attended to.

When the show ends around 5:00 P.M., we immediately begin preparing for the free public concert on the beach. The tents are cleared of all air show guests, and temporary fence is installed to maintain the integrity of the private VIP hospitality area. Shortly thereafter, it is time to get the talent on stage to perform. There now exists the rare opportunity to rest for a short while. Our next responsibility isn't until the concert is winding down, about 75 minutes later.

At this point a military jet is making a series of passes over the crowd as the band is winding up its set. We are in radio contact with the pilot of the jet and the air boss, who keeps us aware of the direction from which the jet will make its next pass and how many passes remain, as well as the fireworks operator and the sound engineer, who are awaiting a cue to simultaneously begin the fireworks display and the accompanying music track once the pilot is safely out of fireworks blast range. The day is completed with a staff meeting to recap the day's events and anticipate any new challenges for the final show day. The day ends somewhere in the neighborhood of 1:00 A.M., which allows us, if we hurry, to sneak in three hours of sleep or so.

The Sunday show is much like the Saturday show with absence of the concert. Despite the shorter day from a time standpoint, the Sunday show seems to take infinitely longer. Between the long days, the unrelenting heat, and the lack of sleep, 5:00 P.M. cannot come quickly enough.

As orderly and strictly controlled as the load-in process is, the load-out procedure requires considerably less order. While a few vendors leave after the show on Sunday, most of them load out on Monday morning as we tear down and load out from the outer borders inward.

Pulling off an event for over four million people takes an experienced team of vendors and, more important, a solid organizational plan to manage all the moving parts. While a super-complex event such as this takes a large team of people to put together, we approach every event, down to the smallest, with the same management style because every successful event is first well organized.

The most important tool to managing the plan for your vendors is the load-in/load-out schedule. This schedule puts everyone (vendors, staff, and venue) on the same page. It also (hopefully) pinpoints issues and problems *before* the event so that they can be addressed and solved. Putting a load-in/load-out schedule together requires only common sense and a logical sense of timing.

When you're on site, the two most important tools at your disposal are communication and a comprehensive staff handbook. Whether you manage your event with cell phones or radios, you'll need to have a quick (or immediate, which is better) way to reach a vendor or a staff member to put out any fires. It is crucial to be able to reach your vendors or any talent on site. Having a work number to call won't help. Whenever possible, we get cell phone numbers, and on site, all key people get a radio. Radios don't have to be fancy with repeaters to reach across the city. They can be the very simple ones that you can buy at any electronics store.

The staff handbook (which we detail later) is simply all the vital information for your event in one packet of papers. It's a small version of your event book that is easily carried around and quickly referenced. The information you include in the staff handbook enables your team and sets them up for success.

Load-In/Load-Out

As you begin to contract and schedule your vendors, you can build your load-in and load-out schedule. You'll need to coordinate your vendors in such a way that they comply with any venue rules and city ordinances, stay out of everybody's way, and then load out in the same manner.

Working backwards through time is the best way to organize your load-in schedule. Based on the start time of your event, you'll want all load-in and setup complete at least a half hour before guests are schedule to arrive. Next, ask who should be in first? Whoever takes the longest to set up should arrive first. For example, if you're in a tent, the tent and floor go in first, then your sound and lighting, then equipment rentals and caterer, and then your decor. If your space is a hotel ballroom, you'll most likely begin with sound and lighting first. If you're in a space that comes equipped with all your sound and lighting equipment, then you'll need your decor first.

The idea is to start with the space you're working in and coordinate with your vendors for load-in times. Somewhere in all that you'll need to work in sound checks as you're able to do them. Last things to arrive are your valet service, registration areas, outside staffing (coat check, attendants, etc.), and entertainment.

For load-out after the event, we usually like everyone to be ready to tear down and load out right away. Load-out always takes less time than load-in. Your vendors can work around each other for load-out and therefore can all arrive at the event end time.

Some things make load-out easier. For example, you'll want your floral vendors to load out right away because of breakable items and because centerpieces sometimes go missing. In addition, your linen company will have a smoother, faster load-out if the tables are clear. Load-out is always easier the sooner you can get your equipment rentals out of the room. Once the room is clear of tables, chairs, and staging, everyone has a lot more space to work. If you know your crowd is slow to leave, be sure to communicate this to your vendors. Also, if you know that the party will go past the scheduled end time, let your vendors know this as well. If your venue has the space and staff to store decor, linens, containers, and other items from your event for you, you may want to schedule to have such items picked up the next day. A normal delivery time (not in the middle of the night or on a Sunday) at your vendor's convenience can save you money on delivery/pickup fees. Most hotels are willing to pull linens from tables and store them for a day or two.

Communications

The key ingredient to the smooth execution of your party is communication. This process of you conducting this orchestra of vendors requires a great amount of communication between each and every vendor. You'll find that at times you'll need to be the go-between and exchange information for them, but this is actually what you want. You want all information to go through you because *you* need to know about all the pieces of this puzzle.

When it comes to coordinating vendors on site, you need to have a communications plan in place. We always use radios. Others may rely on cell phones, but radios are immediate and will save your feet! If your event is a large one, or if it takes place in several locations (different rooms, different floors, inside and outside), renting radios for you, your staff, and your vendors will save your life. Questions can be asked and answered over the radio without you having to run from one place to another. Essentially, with great communications equipment, you can be in more than one place at a time and conduct the building of your event.

Radios on site do not replace the need for complete contact information on all your vendors and talent. We always request a cell phone number not just for our main contact person but also for the person who will be responsible on site. You'll want as much contact information as they'll give you. When it comes to entertainment, we want to know how we're going to be able to reach the talent. Some agen-

EVENT SUCCESS STORY:
THE WORLD'S LARGEST BABY SHOWER

We were on location with 640 pregnant moms-to-be…and this event was to remain a *surprise*! Just to make it interesting, the celebration involved Cindy Crawford, Ben Affleck, Elle McPherson, Sharon Stone, Heather Locklear, Denise Richards, Martina McBride, and Kenny Chesney, and of course, the host Oprah Winfrey. The Oprah Show was going to Fort Campbell Military Base in Kentucky and we were challenged to transform the 101st Airborne's war memorial lawn into a full-scale outdoor theater, complete with seating for 700, three LED screens, 11 camera positions, full set dressing, and backstage support.

Operations is always a huge part of what we do, as it affects every production and how it is executed. We were also responsible for all communications and negotiations with the public affairs office at the base. This included satisfying the needs of the commander of health by providing full on-site medical support for the special needs of this prenatal audience. Production required our team to be on base for over three weeks prior to filming; coordinating shipments, storage, and distribution of all of Oprah's famous prizes.

Throughout this period, we utilized military personnel as part of our production staff to adhere to army protocol and security requirements, which enabled us to pull off this production perfectly. The show aired on October 11, 2004 kicking off network sweeps and received the highest rating of a live show.

Operation baby shower. *(PWEE Staff.)*

cies won't hand over their client's phone numbers, but it never hurts to ask. If you can't get a cell phone number from the agency, then get your agent's cell phone numbers.

Make sure that you have a way to contact every person who is supposed to be working at your event. In this way, when you have a vendor who is supposed to arrive by 6:00 P.M., and you look at your watch at 6:10 P.M., you can call that vendor on his cell phone and find out where he is. Don't ever wait until 6:20 or 6:30 P.M.; instead, stay on top of every arrival, or you could end up with a domino effect of lateness.

Event Handbook

We generate two handbooks that sometimes are bound in book form and sometimes are just a packet of information. Either works. We have one for our staff and one for our vendors. These handbooks are essential on site, but there is a difference in content between the staff and the vendor handbooks. Drawing from the information in your event book (from Chapter 3), you'll want to pull the essential pages that your staff will need to access on site. Our staff handbooks always have the following pages:

- Contact Sheet
- Load-In/Load-Out Schedule
- Event Timeline
- Floor Plan
- Menu

We do the same order every time because the pages are in order according to frequency of use. The "Contact Sheet" is *the* most important page. Your event does not happen without these contact numbers. Of course, for each event, different pages are added. For example, at a complicated event that occurs over multiple days or in several locations or involves a large amount of staff, we'll include call times for groups or volunteers, attire, and staff assignments.

Based on your event, you should gauge what you feel is most important. The last thing you'll want to do is lug around your big event book to access information and then end up misplacing it. You're better off bringing your event book to the site, leaving it in your car or in an office, and then using the staff handbook.

Your vendor handbooks probably will differ from vendor to vendor. Three things are always in a vendor handbook:

- Your (and your staff's) Contact Information
- Load-In/Load-Out Schedule
- Event Timeline

You want to leave as little to chance as possible. Because of this, you should make yourself as accessible (by providing phone numbers) as possible to your vendors while loading in, during the event, and while loading out. All questions should be brought to you because only you have the full picture of what's happening. At the same time, informed vendors make for better service. Giving them a general overview of the event is helpful for them in counseling you.

Lastly, you'll need to provide your venue with a load-in/load-out schedule as well as the event timeline. Having all the key parties (staff, vendors, and venue) informed of the schedule ahead of time is the right time to know if your schedule is workable. Get feedback. Check and double-check that the timing works for everyone. In this way, by the event day, you've given yourself the best chance for a smoothly run event.

Staffing and Volunteers

Staff makes any event go. Volunteers make large events go. There is a significant difference between staff and volunteers. Staff people are usually recruited from your department or office, whereas volunteers are recruited from the general public. Whether your event is of average size and you have a few people on site to help out or your event is large and you have a sizable staff and a bevy of volunteers, your staffing plan will help to keep you organized on site.

148

Estimating Your Staffing Needs

Adequate staff is necessary not just for the event but also for load-in and load-out. It's hard being in two or three places at once, so having staff to help with coordinating logistics will be the key to keeping your sanity. The three critical tools you'll use to determine how much staff you'll need are your load-in/load-out schedule, your event timeline, and your floor plan.

Checking out your load-in schedule, we're sure that there are many times when you have more than one vendor arriving with equipment or product for the event. Each one of your vendors will need to check in and then begin their process of de-

EVENT SUCCESS STORY:
HAVE A BACKUP PLAN FOR EMERGENCIES

To celebrate the grand opening of Chicago's Museum of Contemporary Art, we produced 14 events over 10 days. We knew that we were crazy for taking on a major museum opening while planning all the entertainment for the Athlete Village of the centennial Olympic Games ~ but both events were too great to pass up. We had survived 10 of the 12 events, including a 25-hour public event (Summer Solstice), and with only two events remaining, our team, was exhausted, but kept on going. We decided on the night of an extremely successful black tie gala that raised over $400,000 for the museum that we should get a head start and stay to prepare the tent for the Art World Party event the following evening. We redesigned the lighting, reset the tables and chairs, turned over the linens, and literally did everything we could to allow the team to get a couple hours of extra sleep the next morning.

We had a 2:00 P.M. call that day and arrived at the tent to find that the air-conditioning company had taken our A/C units to another job. It was the end of June, we had record heat, and were left with a potential disaster. The museum had gotten so much of its rentals donated for the events that when the A/C company contracted a paying customer, they moved on to that job. What should we do? What would we do for a location? The event start-time was only four hours away! We moved the entire party set up, including rentals, linens, chairs, into the museum. So much for getting a head start!

No space inside the museum was large enough to accommodate the number of guests coming to the party, so we used two spaces, the theater stage and the theater lobby, to hold the sit-down dinner inside. We refocused all the lighting and custom gobos; reset the kitchen, which had already been set up outside, and moved all the trees and floral arrangements. When the guests began to arrive, we couldn't believe that we had actually gotten it done. All that organization in advance and all that planning ended up pulling away with the A/C units that morning, but we banded together and made it work, while still managing to be dressed appropriately for the black tie event.

The completed look moved from the tent to the lobby and stage inside the museum. *(PWEE Staff.)*

EVENT SUCCESS STORY:
LET YOUR VOLUNTEERS PLAY TO THEIR STRENGTHS

When we were producing the seventy-fifth anniversary event for a large Chicago-based snack food maker, we encountered great success with using volunteer committees. The plant's long-standing relationship with its neighbors, as well as the family-oriented nature of the company, made holding the events on plant property an easy decision. The day of the anniversary events began with a block party and rarely offered plant tours geared toward the associates and their families, as well as the community. The events culminated with a VIP gala that evening, held in a giant tent on plant property.

To allow the associates to feel more involved in the event, we set up various committees to allow those interested to give their input and feel more included. The committees we created were Invitations/RSVP Management, Parking and Security, Internal Communications, Tours, Family Day Block Party, and Photo/Video. The use of committees was instrumental to the success of the event.

Despite the company's close relationship with its neighbors, much of its history, as well as its current operations, remained shrouded in secrecy. The tour committee was able to create a quick but interesting glimpse inside the plant for the over 4,500 employees and their families who came for the tours.

The photo/video committee was able to get us access to a multitude of archived photographs and commercials that were used as decor at the event and in the specially created DVD. This custom DVD served as the giveaway for the guests at the VIP event and was featured in their newly created museum.

The invitation committee helped design the invitation and was then responsible for sending out the invitations, as well as keeping the RSVP list, which it updated on a weekly basis. The

committee also was very familiar with the large group of retirees who were invited and was able to handle a long list of special arrangements requested by them. The committees were able to provide easier and greater access to company resources while assisting our team in maintaining the integrity of the company's principles and standards in every aspect of the celebration.

Associates and their families line up for a tour of the plant. *(John Reilly Photography.)*

livering its equipment and setting it up as well. Thus, if it's 10:00 A.M. and your sound and lighting company is set to arrive at the dock to unload but your catering company is arriving at the same time to unload at the front entrance. You'll need a staff person to meet one of these vendors. Check the rest of your load-in schedule. What other times are similar to this? Don't be afraid to delegate. If you have radios to communicate with your staff and vendors, then you can still keep a handle on everything that's going on.

When going through your event timeline, you'll want the same people who interacted with vendors to then be in charge of those elements for your event. For example, if you had one person who was in charge of checking in the valet company, the attendants for coat check and bathrooms, as well as the delivery of the giveaways, you'll then want that same person to oversee those elements during the event. That person would make sure that valet ran smoothly and quickly, he or she would make sure that your bathroom attendants and coat check people were in place for guests, and then he or she would be responsible for setting up the giveaway tables at the end of the evening. The one thing you must keep in mind is that some responsibilities can overlap with timing, so be sure that you haven't spread your staff too thin either.

Load-out is the easiest. Be sure that your vendors are on time to tear down, and then just let them go. They will have it covered, and you won't need as much staff. Staff responsibilities for load-out usually involve making sure that items used for the event get back to the office. For example, if you had a silent auction, you'll have lots of display items, clipboards, pens, and so on. Assign one or two people to clean up that area, box up your supplies, and get them back to your office. The same can be done for any leftover giveaways, programs, awards, or paperwork.

Once you have an idea of how many people you want to help you on site, then decide when you want them to arrive and how long you'll need them there for you. All this information will go in your staff handbooks that you will give to each person.

If your event is large, such as a festival or a fund-raiser with 500 people and many elements, you may need to have volunteers. Volunteers make terrific greeters, people movers, and docents. They don't, however, always work well to assist during load-in or load-out because they're not usually privy to a lot of the background information needed at those times. Moreover, you never want to ask too much of your volunteers. These people are giving their time, and as such, you really shouldn't demand extensive work hours or taxing jobs that may be boring and hard.

If you have any event where your guests have a silent auction or they move from space to space (say, from one room for cocktails to a ballroom for dinner and then to a theater for a show), volunteers are wonderful at helping direct people to the next space, to the restrooms, or to the valet and coat check. Volunteers are also terrific for registration (make sure that you have a staff person present to oversee), for giveaways, or to hand out programs. You want to find simple, easy tasks that are fairly quick.

Training and Appreciation

A well-run event has a proficient staff and thinking volunteers. What makes your team proficient? Informed, effective training, trust, and thorough information at their fingertips. In other words, you need to provide the tools to your team that will help them succeed.

Training begins long before the event. After you have your staff handbook ready, you'll want to hold a preproduction staff meeting. We usually do it about a week before the event. This meeting is the time to distribute the staff handbook; go over the details of the event; discuss responsibilities, attire, and call times; and field questions. This step in the training process is crucial before the event because inevitably someone comes up with a glitch in your plan, and you can solve that problem prior to the event.

Training for volunteers may happen before the event, but usually you should provide them with materials before the event and then do a quick run-through when they arrive at the event. The minimum information you'll need to provide your volunteer staff before the event is

- Description of Job
- Appropriate Attire
- Call Time
- Common Questions
- Who to Ask for Help
- Event Timeline
- Floor Plan

These points are just the common denominator for volunteer handbooks. You may want to add more information that discusses the specific needs of your event.

These two steps are taken before the event. At your event it's a good idea to do a quick meeting with everyone. You should have a staff meeting early in the day so that you can point out any changes and answer any last-minute questions. Also,

EVENT SUCCESS STORY: TREAT YOUR VOLUNTEERS WELL

Volunteers are a crucial part of an event's success whether they are handling registration, auction area management, reservations, giveaways, greeting guests, moving people, acting as docents, staffing water stations, giving participants directions along a race route, or doing cash management. It is very important to keep in mind that volunteers are giving their time and are not getting paid for their efforts. Therefore, you should always try to commit more volunteers than you think you'll need to make up for the inevitable scheduling conflicts and no-shows.

It is also important to schedule volunteers in two- to three-hour shifts, not asking too much of them or their time. Their jobs should be basic in nature and their directives very clear so that one person can fill in for another. Because of the charitable nature, fund-raising events have the greatest need for volunteers.

For an annual five-kilometer run/walk that attracted over 25,000 participants, we handled all the event logistics and operations, including race management, street closures, city services, permitting, vendor and sponsor support, construction of the team village, event program, and most important, volunteer management. For an event of this size, we needed over 1,000 volunteers.

They assisted with runner and walker registration, packet pickup, pledge office, and water stations and were placed all along the route to help the 25,000 runner and walker participants find their way. We had multiple training sessions with the volunteer team captains, and each team leader had an area of responsibility and a team of volunteers to execute their needs. We provided them with a procedure packet giving them a map of the sponsor area, a map of the route, a list of shift assignments for their area, arrival and direction procedures, and a list of answers to frequently asked questions, as well as a radio to get to the right person for any additional questions or special requests. This event that has been taking place for over 13 years, raising $2.5 million, would never be possible without the help of volunteers.

Twenty-five thousand participants gather on Mother's Day every year to help fight breast cancer. *(John Reilly Photography.)*

make sure that everyone who is supposed to have a radio has a radio and knows how to use it. You probably have a staff person in charge of the volunteer team, so as each volunteer arrives, he or she will need a quick rundown of the event layout and instructions on where to go. Volunteer responsibilities should be fairly simple, and their shifts should be as short as possible.

We believe that a key ingredient to successful events is respect. If you show respect and appreciation for your staff, volunteers, crew, and vendors, then as a team you will be able to overcome almost *any* challenge. It is so important to let your staff—particularly volunteers because they don't have to be there—know how much you appreciate them. If you follow the basic kindergarten sandbox rule, you can't go wrong. Treat them how you would like to be treated.

- Give them plenty of breaks.
- Be sure to feed them, and make sure that they have plenty of water or something to drink.
- Short shifts or changes of pace will keep them stimulated and interested.
- Show respect.
- If you can, have enough of the giveaway bags so that they can have one too. It doesn't have to be the guest giveaway bag, but a token of appreciation goes a long way.
- Release staff as soon as you can.
- Say it as often as you think it, "Thank you, thank you, thank you." Be sure they know their value to you, your sanity, and your event.

Tips for Staffing Success

- Make the shifts for your volunteers as short as possible.
- Have a staff meeting before the event and one during load-in.
- Put your best staff up front, dealing with guests.
- Recruit more volunteers than you think you will need. Having too much help is usually better than being short of help.
- Match your load-in assignments with event assignments. For example, if one person is in charge of checking in the entertainment, it should be his or her job during the event to make sure that the entertainment's breaks are at the right time, that they have their hospitality, and so on.
- Don't forget to say "Please" and "Thank you." Your approach with staff and volunteers will make or break *their* experience.

Security

For event planning, when we talk about security, we don't necessarily mean a six-foot, five-inch off-duty police officer at the door. When it comes to security for private events, we're really talking about liability issues. You need to be concerned about the safety of your guests, protecting the space, and insurance. Adequate security is necessary at any event, and it really comes in different forms. Security includes credentialing, registration procedures, access, and responsibility for equipment.

For large public events or high-profile events with public figures—such as festivals, hospitality villages, or grand openings—where you've involved city or county services, closed a public street, or are expecting thousands of people, security does involve an outside firm. And yes, it also involves many six-foot, five-inch off-duty police officers. A good security plan for a public event also includes emergency medical personnel, permitting site modifications (fencing, etc.), and even a threat assessment. Don't be overwhelmed. If you have a large event, you'll be hiring a professional security firm who will provide you with these elements in its security plan. If you have a smaller event and are putting together your own security, we've outlined a few key areas for you to consider.

When bringing the President through the Athlete Village, our private security team assisted President Clinton's security team, the Secret Service. *(Sam Bryant.)*

EVENT SUCCESS STORY:
SECURITY IS CRUCIAL FOR ALL TYPES OF EVENTS

When planning an event of a certain magnitude, we insist on developing a professional, comprehensive security/crowd-control plan. The plan must be very clear yet seem unobtrusive and almost an invisible part of our overall event plan to the guest.

The possibility for disruptive and unlawful activity exists at all major public and private events and should be anticipated, and planned for, with a response plan. This allows for there to be as little disruption to the event as possible, where the guests might not even notice that something has happened. The size, profile, and guest list for an event determines how much security is needed and what kind of plan needs to be in place. Events may require that you work with hotel security, city departments, or even the Secret Service. If you have a complicated, multilayered security plan and team, you can be prepared for numerous last-minute changes.

During a series of grand opening events for a major hospital, we were thrilled to have former First Lady Hillary Rodham Clinton agree to be part of our dedication ceremony. While we had worked with many political figures and their security teams before, working with the Secret Service detail for the First Lady was a very different experience. Due to the nature of the person in protection, it makes sense that their security measures would include lots of last minute changes requiring us to fundamentally replan an entire event that took six months to produce, all in just 24 hours before the ceremony was set to kick off.

We had a security and crowd-control plan in place when the Secret Service advance team arrived for their walk through. By the end of the site survey we had to change the location of the stage, change the type of podium we were using, add tent walls along her entrance walk (to protect against a sniper attack), relocate all of the rope and stanchion, change our access routes, and change our traffic plan. Our production timeline that morning went from setup and done to completely starting over, as well as needing to get the names, Social Security Numbers, birthdates, and birth cities from every person working the following day. *That* was a last minute vetting process. All of the changes and through-the-night working was worth it because the hospital received a tremendous amount of national and local publicity directly attributed to the First Lady's participation in the dedication ceremony.

Since then, we have encountered numerous Secret Service advance team visits for charity events, grand openings, and private events and have learned that you have your plan in place, with built-in time for the list of expected changes. When we produced a presidential library grand opening, we managed the vetting process for all the 1,000 VIP attendees at the ceremony, as well as anyone working within 100 feet of the stage. And, as part of the security plan, we had garbage cans along the motorcade route removed, manhole covers welded shut, rooftop access restricted, and even air traffic diverted. We worked around the bomb dogs' schedule, snipers, and countless numbers of Secret Service officers in front of the stage, backstage, and in some cases on the stage. With a preliminary plan in place, the whole team understands that you're experienced, and the process is less painful. Rather than looking at changes as an ordeal, we view them as a challenge and approach solving them in that way.

Bomb dogs inspect the stage area before the grand opening ceremony. *(John Reilly Photography.)*

Even when we aren't working with the Secret Service on a job, there is a heightened sense of security that needs to be addressed at all public and high profile events. During the grand opening of a convention center, we had to prepare for protestors who planned to picket the grand opening gala. The protestors got their permit, and planted themselves right in front of the doors of the convention center and along the red carpet for guest arrivals. Because we had anticipated this issue and had concocted a solution with the local authorities we were able to make a single phone call to have the protestors moved to their legal, permitted location, down the street, and about a block away from the red carpet gala entrance. With the right amount of planning, and good communication, our issue became a nonissue.

Understanding Liability Issues

At special events, when people discuss security, they are thinking liability. As the producer, you will need to make sure that both your vendors and your venue are secure should anything happen at your party. We kind of figure it like this. If something can fall, catch fire, or make guests sick, you need to get insurance from that vendor. The most common vendors we request additional insurance from are

- Sound and lighting firms
- Caterers
- Valet services
- Security firms
- Decor companies

It is part of their job to help you make your event safe and secure for your guests and for the venue. Each applicable vendor should name you (or your company), as well as the venue, as additionally insured for any load-in or load-out days, as well as the event date. They should then provide you with a copy of that certificate of insurance that you will then keep in your event book. If you're not sure if you need insurance from a vendor, ask for it. Better to be safe than sorry.

Obtaining the certificate of insurance is a very simple process. Because we're regularly asking for these certificates, we actually send out a form e-mail or fax to all the pertinent vendors listing the entities to be named on the certificate and requesting that a copy be sent to us. The same could be accomplished by asking for it over the phone as well. Having a vendor name you or your venue as additionally insured on the certificate should not cost anything extra to you.

You also should ask for insurance from your venue for you or your company. Just for extra coverage, we like to be named on our venue's insurance as well. Seeing that the event itself is covered by our permanently held event insurance, we like to be covered by the venue for extra protection. Accidents can happen, so it's nice to know that if anyone ever needed it, we have plenty of insurance (from us, from vendors, and from the venue) to provide a resolution to most problems.

Credentials

The best start to a good security plan is good credentials for your guests, staff, and vendors. Credentials come in all sorts of forms. For elegant events, we've used pins. For big events, we use lanyards or wristbands. For formal events, we usually just ask the guests to bring their invitation. For themed events, credentials can do double duty as a giveaway. For example, at a beach party, we may give each guest a custom lanyard with a lifeguard whistle.

Credentials don't have be boring or even official looking; they just need to be visible and hard to duplicate. Guests aren't always the only ones to get credential passes. At large events with several different access areas, you can have more security and put credentials on the vendor crews, the entertainment, and even you

This credential (one of six types distributed) has large print and the date and is color-coded to make it easier for security to identify who belongs where within a secure area. *(Created by Award Vision.)*

and your staff. With everyone having different credentials with different levels of access, it makes it very easy for security to identify who belongs where.

Protecting the Space and Protecting Your Guests

Your event may not require security. That's okay; don't feel that you have to hire security. But your venue may require it. When your venue requires that you hire security, it is requesting personnel to protect the space, not your guests.

Venues such as museums, arenas, stadiums, and historical sites may have an in-house security team that you will be have to pay for. These security people are there to monitor your guests' activities and secure the space, art, or artifacts of the location. These security personnel are not there to prevent party crashers, secure rented equipment, escort uninvited guests out, or help with a medical situation. If you feel that you want a staff of security to help you with these types of things at your event, you will need to hire an outside security firm. For large events or high-profile public events, you may want to consider hiring the firm to consult on your security plan, as well as provide you with the personnel.

Finding a Security Firm

Finding a good security firm is just like looking for any other kind of vendor (check out Chapter 3). The hardest part is knowing where to start. One good place is with your venue. If your venue requires extra security, ask for a reference or two. Another good place to start is with another vendor with whom you already have a relationship, one that you trust. If you can get together a couple of names of security firms, you can then meet with them face to face, get a proposal, and check references. We prefer security firms that include plenty of police officers (off duty, on duty, retired) on their staff and firms that have strong relationships with the police department and any city/county departments. Beyond those criteria, screen them like you would any other vendor.

Security always has been important to successful event planning, but it has become even more critical since the September 11 attacks. Terrorism is a new and real concern for us, and while it is unlikely to occur at an event, most event planners and their clients aren't taking any chances. Gone are the days when security was viewed as a precaution to manage crowds and diffuse tense situations. Today, the entire nature of security has changed, especially for events that are complex in nature and involve large crowds in public areas.

As a company that plans and executes extremely complex events, we always have been attuned to the need for extra security at most of our events. These days, not only has the sense of urgency for security increased, but it is now also recognized as a wise investment even at the smallest of affairs.

Tips for a Safe Event

- Do you have more than 750 guests? You may want to consider hiring an emergency medical team to be at your event.
- Do you have a lot of guests in a remote area or far from the nearest hospital? You may want to consider hiring an EMT with a dedicated ambulance.
- Is your event high profile, a public event, or do your guests include dignitaries or celebrities? You probably should hire a security firm to put a security plan together for you and then execute it.
- Make your credentials easy to identify for your security people, and make them fun with creative ideas for your guests.
- Put your best, smartest staff and volunteers at registration.
- Put credentials on guests, staff, volunteers, crews, and entertainment.
- Pinpoint areas of concern during your site visit, and address solutions early.
- Get insurance certificates from your vendors, and have them name you (or your company) as additionally insured.
- Your hired security firm should have strong ties to city services and city government (such as the police department, department of transportation, and the mayor's office).

7

Step Seven:
Post Event Follow-Up

You're basking in the afterglow of a successful, fun event. Your feet hurt, you haven't eaten anything but a few hors d'oeuvres on the run, you've taken off your radio (yet you can still hear voices in your head), and now you just want to sit down, take your shoes off, and relax. Maybe next week.

You have three hurdles to clear before this event is officially closed. You need to account for overages (if any), do a post event evaluation, and write and send your thank-you letters. This chapter covers these three crucial post event activities.

Budget Overages

Any event can (and usually does) have unforeseen challenges. Because of this, you can end up with overages. Therefore, even though you've paid all your vendors in full on the event day, there may be some additional charges. The key is that you should have been notified of any extras as they occurred. For example, if you accidentally didn't order enough linens, your linen crew should have told you as soon as they found out and then asked you if you wanted to rent more linens or take away tables. If you order extra linens, you'll be paying extra rental charges. If the linen crew accidentally forgot to bring some of the linens, then it's the linen company's financial responsibility to make up the difference.

Another common overage is with entertainment. If your party goes longer than you estimated (and budgeted), then you have the choice to either cut the music or ask for overtime. If you decide to keep your band, then there is an overtime charge for the musicians. When you negotiated and contracted with your entertainment, they should let you know (and you should ask) what the overtime costs are. Based on the extra charge, you then can decide to keep the band for an extra half hour or for however long they're willing to stay and you're willing to pay.

Whatever challenges your event presented, the best time to deal with overages is the day after (or the Monday after) the event. The event is still fresh in your mind, all your paperwork can be organized and incorporated into your event book, and you can then revise your budget to its final version.

Sometimes you have a situation where your vendor knows that there will be overages, but he isn't sure how much. Don't wait for the vendor to call you. Reach out to the vendor immediately after and get those numbers! You want the vendor to get his final invoice together while the event is fresh in his mind as well. We've found that as time goes by, people tend to forget the details of what happened at an event, and forgetting details can be financially dodgy to your budget. Stay on top of your vendors, and stay disciplined. Aim to have your budget finalized within a day or two of the event.

Post Event Evaluation

Once you've paid all your vendors in full, you should have your final budget done. Now you're ready to do your post event evaluation. If event planning is not for you, obviously you don't need to do this step. If, on the other hand, you do want to plan other events, doing a postmortem on your party will be so valuable to the overall experience—and to all your future projects.

To do the evaluation, you'll need to make two lists. The first list to write down is "Areas of Improvement," and the second is "What Went Right."

We like to finish on a positive note, so we always begin with "Areas of Improvement." Be honest. Be brutally honest. Especially with your own performance. *Every* event, not most, but every single event, without exception, can be improved. Here are some questions to ask yourself:

- Was everyone on time?
- Were there lines at the food stations?
- How about the bars?
- How was the sound?
- Did you have enough lighting?
- Was your budget realistic?
- Did the event run itself?
- Was there enough security? Was there too much security?
- What did you miss?
- How did the decor look?
- Was there enough seating? Was there too much seating?
- Did the flowers look dead at the end of the event?
- How many centerpieces did the guests take that weren't supposed to be taken?
- In what condition did you leave the venue?
- What wasn't perfect?

You need to be objective and consider if the problem could have been avoided, and if it could, where was the breakdown in communication? Or who dropped the ball and why? If you had a problem that could not have been foreseen, how do you avoid it in the future? This last part is the most valuable part of a post event evaluation. How do you do better in the future? This is why we love event production. There's always a new challenge, and there's always something new to learn.

After you've torn apart your event, you get to pour on the praises. Make sure that you send plenty by way of your vendors. To begin the process of making your "What Went Right" list, keep alongside that your list of fantastic vendors. When you've finished cataloguing what was good about your event, you'll also have made your list of thank-you notes to send out. Again, be honest, because when you look at what was great, you'll want to remember that and learn from what you did right as well. Hopefully, at the end of this process, your list of problems won't be too long, and even if is, your guests may or may not have noticed any of them.

Thank You

We like to send a thank-you note to every first-time vendor who did a great job. Such notes sometimes can be hard to write, so we've included a sample or two in

Appendix A. Don't send a thank-you note by e-mail. Always mail one, and if your event is small (such as a small party at your home), a hand-written note can be nice. If your event is large (such as the company holiday party for 100 people or more), you'll want to send a typed thank-you letter on company letterhead. Taking the time to thank your vendors is the beginning to building a good, long-standing relationship with your vendors or venue. It demonstrates and encourages loyalty between the two of you. It also will demonstrate your appreciation, which, as we know from working with volunteers, can go a long way.

If you and your vendors have mutual respect and loyalty, then when there are really big problems, such as your 60-foot stage slowly being submerged in the high tide, you'll have someone to rely on. Some of the best solutions for problems come from a vendor who has nothing to do with the problem to begin with.

Producing events is a team project and a team effort. Cultivate this atmosphere by never taking advantage, never taking your team for granted, always acknowledging their contribution, showing your appreciation, and *always, always* saying please and thank you.

Appendix A:
Forms

Contact Sheet

Contact List

Client

Name	Chicago phone	123 456 7890
Address	Chicago fax	123 456 7890
	Springs phone	123 456 7890
	Springs fax	123 456 7890
	Toronto	123 456 7890
Company Information/Contact	phone	123 456 7890
Address	fax	123 456 7890

Venue

Rental Events Manager	direct	123 456 7890
City, State Zip	fax	123 456 7890
	email	x@venue.com
Operations Assistant	direct	123 456 7890
	Fax	123 456 7890
	e-mail	x@operations.com
In-House Catering	phone	123 456 7890
	fax	123 456 7890
	e-mail	x@catering.com
Contact	direct	123 456 7890

Entertainment

Entertainment Company	phone	123 456 7890
	fax	123 456 7890
	e-mail	x@entertainment.com
String Quartet	phone	123 456 7890
	fax	123 456 7890
Production Company	phone	123 456 7890
Human Decor	home	123 456 7890
	fax	123 456 7890
	e-mail	x@production.com
Guitarist	phone	123 456 7890
	fax	123 456 7890

Vendors

Signage	phone	123 456 7890
	fax	123 456 7890
Cake	phone	123 456 7890
	fax	123 456 7890
Catering	phone	123 456 7890
	e-mail	x@catering.com
Calligraphy	phone	123 456 7890
	fax	123 456 7890
Hotel	main	123 456 7890
	fax	123 456 7890
Custom Staging	work	123 456 7890
	fax	123 456 7890
	cell	123 456 7890
Sound	phone	123 456 7890
	fax	123 456 7890
	page	123 456 7890
Limousines	toll free	123 456 7890
	phone	123 456 7890
	fax	123 456 7890
Lighting	phone	123 456 7890
	fax	123 456 7890
	cell	123 456 7890
	page	123 456 7890
Security	phone	123 456 7890
	fax	123 456 7890
	page	123 456 7890
	cell	123 456 7890
Hotel	phone	123 456 7890
	fax	123 456 7890

169

Valet		phone	123 456 7890
		fax	123 456 7890
		cell	123 456 7890
Floral Company		phone	123 456 7890
		fax	123 456 7890
		home	123 456 7890
		cell	123 456 7890
Photography		phone	123 456 7890
		fax	123 456 7890
		cell	123 456 7890
Calligraphy		phone	123 456 7890
		fax	123 456 7890
		additional	123 456 7890
Linens		phone	123 456 7890
		cell	123 456 7890

Event Timelines

Birthday Event Timeline

6:45 P.M.   Valet in place on Michigan Avenue
Tuxedoed security in place
Ushers to open center doors for guests
Greeters to welcome guests and direct them to the rotunda
Human decor in place
Strings to form promenade in arcade (until 7:20 P.M.)
Waitstaff to offer trays of champagne in the arcade
Elevator and bathroom attendants in place

7:00 P.M.   Guests begin to arrive
Food stations and bars open in rotunda
Waitstaff to pass hors d'oeuvres
Background Jazz performs

7:55 P.M.   Emcee to introduce grandchildren (on staircase, youngest at the top)
Grandchildren to sing "Happy Birthday"

8:00 P.M.   Emcee asks everyone to please join the family for dinner
PWEE staff to assist with people moving
Greeters to assist guests at the foyer
Ushers to open doors for guests
Greeters to escort guests up the stage stairs and assist with seating
Strings performing from balcony

8:20 P.M.   Guests seated
First course preset, waitstaff to pass bread and serve wines

8:30 P.M.   Emcee introduces guest of honor to welcome everyone

8:40 P.M.   Emcee introduces guest of honor's son for a toast

8:45 P.M.   Intermezzo served

8:55 P.M.   Emcee introduces guest of honor's second son for a toast

9:00 P.M.	Entrée served
9:15 P.M.	Human decor (with birthday cake hat) in place on foyer stairs Flamenco guitarist on set on round stage in inner lobby Waitstaff ready with champagne on second-level foyer stairs
9:25 P.M.	Emcee introduces guest of honor's third son for a toast
9:30 P.M.	Emcee invites everyone to Grainger Ballroom Flamenco guitarist performs in theater lobby
9:35 P.M.	CD music (Sinatra or Streisand) in ballroom Main bar open and attendants making espresso, latté, and cappuccino made to order Three-tiered confectionery stands set on cocktail tables
10:00 P.M.	Band goes to stage Band begins to perform "Happy Birthday"; everyone sings Caterer to bring out birthday cake
10:05 P.M.	Waitstaff to offer birthday cake as they pass assorted desserts
10:20 P.M.	Emcee to introduce Bobby Short
11:10 P.M.	Flamenco guitarist performs
Midnight	Event ends

Themed Corporate Event Timeline

7:00 P.M.   Guests begin to arrive; woman on stilts greets guests
Waitstaff to pass hors d'oeuvres
Bars open and Mojitos Specialty Bar opens
The Three Grandpas perform on *grand ballroom stage*
The Havana Social Club Sextet perform on *international ballroom stage*
Cigarette girls pass chocolate cigars
Betty Sitbon paints cigar boxes, turning them into purses (*grand ballroom*)
Cigar rollers are rolling cigars (*grand ballroom*)
Mad hatter station opens (*international ballroom*)
Candy sculptor performing (*international ballroom*)
Tattoo artists in both rooms

7:30 P.M.   Bocce ball competition (*international ballroom*)
Chicken Foot Cuban dominoes (*grand ballroom*)
Food stations open

8:00 P.M.   Havana parade begins with big head puppets and human floats, with CEO reveal

8:15 P.M.   Bandoleros perform in *grand ballroom*
Orchestra of the Americas performs in *international ballroom*

9:30 P.M.   Orchestra of the Americas performs (big number along with parade of human floats, women on stilts, and the Ashe Dancers)

10:00 P.M.   Bandoleros perform with dancing in *grand ballroom*

10:15 P.M.   Waitstaff to pass Cuban desserts and *The Havana Post*

Midnight   Event ends

173

Menus

Reception and Seated Dinner

Rotunda 1 & 2
Passed Hors D'oeuvres (A Variety Of Six) As Guests Arrive
Bars Open And Wines And Waters To Be Passed

Mini Sweet Onion Tart
Pear & Brie Quesadilla
Coconut Shrimp Served With Balsamic Apricot Sauce
Curried Vegetable Spring Rolls With Ginger Apricot Sauce & Toasted Sesame Seeds
Beggars Purse Filled With Mushrooms
Corn & Andouille Salsa Tart (Or Sausage En Croute With Stone Ground Mustard)
Mini Potato Crisps Topped With Crème Fraîche & Salmon (Or Mini Potato Pancake Served With
Apple Chutney ~ Or Sweet Potato Fritter With Scallions, Zucchini & Red Pepper Dipping Sauce)
Curried Scallops Seared Golden

Note: If we do not have a sushi station, then I would add California rolls instead of the veggie
spring rolls to the passed hors d'oeuvres.

Food Stations in Rotunda I
Beluga ~ Sevruya & Osetra Caviar Display With Frozen Ketel One Vodka Or Flower Filled Ice
Tower With Assorted Flavored Vodkas
~ Also ~
A Uniformed Chef Carving Scottish Smoked Salmon & A Chef Preparing Buckwheat Blinis

Uniformed Chef Cleaving Whole Crispy Peking Duck
Accompanied By Plum Sauce On Scallion Pancakes

Uniformed Chef Carving Herb Crusted Oven Roasted Ahi Tuna
Accompanied By Wasabi, Chili Fennel Slaw On To Scallion Biscuits

Full Premium Bars

Cabaret Table Seating

Food Stations in Rotunda II

Sushi (From Mirai)
Two Sushi Chefs Dressed In Kimonos Preparing An Assortment Of Fresh Sushi & Sashimi
Spicy Crab Rolls & Assorted Maki Roles Served With Chip Sticks

Dim Sum
From Phoenix Restaurant In China Town
Bruschetta Bar Chefs Preparing To Order

Reception and Seated Dinner

First Course
Lobster Salad In Curried Vinaigrette With Salad Of Fresh Herbs
Individual Ice Carved Vessel With A Taste Of Chilled Melon Soup

Entrée
Grilled Veal Chop
Duchess Potatoes

Option: Chargrilled Tenderloin Of Beef

<u>*Note*</u>*: Coffee & Tea To Be Served In Cabaret (Grand Ballroom) ~*
Also, We Will Need A Vegetarian Option

Desserts
Ballroom To Be Set With 42-36" Rounds ~ Seating Approximately 210 Guests For Cabaret Show
The Centerpiece For Each Table To Be A Tiered Confectionery Stand
Filled With Truffles From Vosges, Fruit Glaces, Cookies, Bittersweet Chocolate Ganache,
Caramelized Nuts, And Other Diminutive Sweets

Butler Passed Desserts
Waitstaff To Pass A Selection Of Individual Demitasse Tastes Of
Crème Brulee (Vanilla, Chocolate & Coffee), Gratin Of Berries With A Champagne Sabayon Sauce,
Variety Of Tarts And Tortes

<u>*Note*</u>*: There is a possibility that we will bring in mini decorated cakes from New York instead of the*
tortes and tarts. We will definitely bring in a birthday cake.

Stations In Grand Ballroom Foyer
Approximately 10:30 P M
Chef To Prepare Bananas Foster

Coffee & Tea Station (Also To Be Served By Waitstaff)

<u>*Note*</u>*: Cappuccino & Espresso Machines At The Bar*

175

Menus

Food Stations

Sushi Station
Master Sushi Chefs Preparing Nigiri Sushi & Maki Rolls
Served With Tamari, Wasabi Mustard & Pickled Ginger To Garnish

Featured Nigiri Sushi
Shrimp, Yellowtail, Salmon, Tuna, Eel & Mackerel

Featured Maki Rolls
Spicy Tuna, California, Alaskan, Yellowtail & Asparagus, Avocado & Cucumber

Shrimp & Vegetable Gyoza
With Chili Scallion Soy Sauce

Beef Negamaki
Scallions Wrapped With Soy Marinated Beef

Pan American Station
Churrasco Carving Station
Marinated Beef, Pork & Lamb Barbequed Gaucho Style
Over A Wood Burning Fire Set On Authentic Gaucho Swords Carved
To Order At The Buffet
Served With Sauces Of Sao Paulo Salsa, Three-Pepper Relish & Chimichum

Valencia Paella
With Shrimp, Minted Chicken Meatballs, Chorizo, Kalamata & Green Onions,
Saffron Rice, Tomato, Onions & Peppers Tossed With Short Grain Rice

Petite Stacks Of Roasted Pork
Set On Polenta Diamonds Layered With Cannelloni Beans, Tomato,
Spinach & Polenta
Finished With Saffron Sauce & A Mediterranean Compote

Vegetable & Beef Empanadas
Served With Salsa Verde & Chipolte Crème

Mango & Jicama Salad
With Scallions, Bean Sprouts, Avocado & Fresh Cilantro
Tossed With A Lime Tequila Dressing

Pacific Rim Station
Uniformed Chef Preparing Scallion Pancakes Filled With Szechuan Duck
With Bowls Of Chopped Peanuts, Scallions & Ginger Hoisin Sauce

Crispy Beef & Vegetable Stir Fry With Oyster Sauce, To Include
Bean Sprouts, Chinese Broccoli, Water Chestnuts, Crispy Peapods,
Wood Ear Mushrooms, Chinese Greens & Scallions Served With Sticky Rice

Vegetarian Thai Summer Rolls
With Bean Sprouts, Carrots, Napa Cabbage & Mint
With A Red Chili Peanut Sauce, Set On Shredded Cabbage

Authentic Crab Rangoons
Set On Rice Noodles With Hot Chinese Mustard Sauce & Plum Sauce

Vietnamese Noodle Salad
With Bok Choy, Peapods, Red Pepper, Broccoli, Cilantro,
Black & White Sesame Seeds,
Crushed Peanuts, Tossed With A Tossed Sesame Vinaigrette

Mediterranean Station
Chef Sautéing Souviaki Marinated Chicken, Lamb & Vegetables
Served To Pita Bread With Tzatziki Sauce & Hot Sauce To The Side

Bedouin Couscous
With Pumpkin, Carrots, Turnips, Sweet Peppers & Chick Peas In A Mild Sauce

Grilled Autumn Vegetable With Thyme Scented Olive Oil
Featuring Portabello Mushroom, Eggplant, Red Pepper,
Green & Yellow Squash, Fennel, Carrots & Green Onion

177

Mediterranean Mezza
Tabbouleh With Hummus, Babaganoush, Olive Tapenade
Served To Toasted Pita Triangles & Flat Bread,

Garnished With Bowls Of Exotic Mediterranean Olive With Herbed Feta Cheese

Vegetarian Persian Domaldes
With Pignoli Tarts, Rice Parsley With Argolemono

Indian Station
Clay Oven Tandori Shrimp
With The Traditional Tandori Spices

Black Gram & Yellow Dal Maharani
Black & Yellow Lentils With Sliced Ginger Root, Cumin Seeds & Garam Masala

Chicken Murgh
Chicken In Rich Saffron Curry With Garlic, Cardamom Pods,
Mixed Nuts & Yogurt

Saffron Scented Jasmine Rice With Mixed Vegetables

Potato & Vegetable Samosas With Madras Curry & Scallions

Nan, Garlic Naan & Herbed Papadum Breads

Desserts & Coffee Station
Chocolate Dipped Banana Toffee Crunch
Fresh Fruit Tartlets
Caramel Apple Tarte Tatin
Individual Cobblers Of Fresh Seasonal Fruit
Petite Chocolate Dipped Apricot Filled Macaroons
Prickly Pear Cactus & Pear Puree Tartlets With Fresh Mint
Petite Chocolate Caramel Finger Brownies
Brie & Apricot Tartlets In Phyllo With Toasted Almonds
Cinnamon-Apple Wontons Dusted With Brown Sugar
Petite Guava-Cream Cheese Turnovers Dusted With Powdered Sugar
Pumpkin Mousse Tartlets With Crumbled Ginger Snaps In Florentine Cups

Regular & Decaffeinated Dark Roast Coffee
Gourmet Black, Green & Herbal Teas
Cream, Sugar, Honey & Sweetener

Dessert Goodie Bag To Go
Placed In An Ornate Bag To Include

Small Sleeves Of Popcorn & Caramel Corn
Bundled Pouch Filled With Dark Chocolate Mint Truffles
Petite Gold Bags Of Maple Sugar Glazed Mixed Nuts
Silver Cellophane Wrapped Chocolate Dipped Strawberries

Floor Plans

Seated Dinner

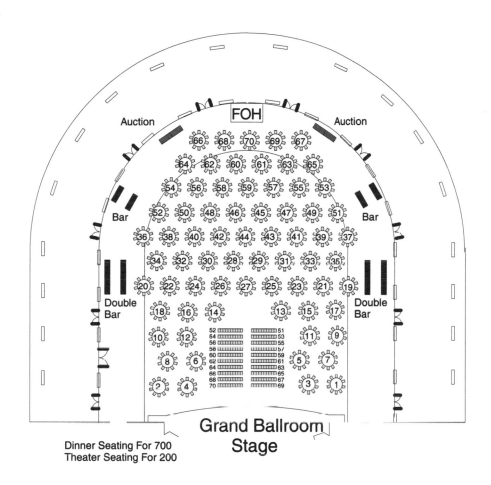

FOH

Auction   Auction

66 68 70 69 67

64 62 60 61 63 65

Bar 54 56 58 59 57 55 53 Bar

52 50 48 46 45 47 49 51

36 38 40 42 44 43 41 39 37

34 32 30 28 29 31 33 35

Double
Bar 20 22 24 26 27 25 23 21 19 Double
Bar

18 16 14   13 15 17

10 12   52   51   11   9
         54   53
         56   55
8   6   58   57   5   7
         60   59
         62   61
2   4   64   63   3   1
         66   65
         68   67
         70   69

Grand Ballroom
Stage

Dinner Seating For 700
Theater Seating For 200

**Gala
Saturday, June 12, 2004
Navy Pier ~ Grand Ballroom**

Floor Plans

Reception Style

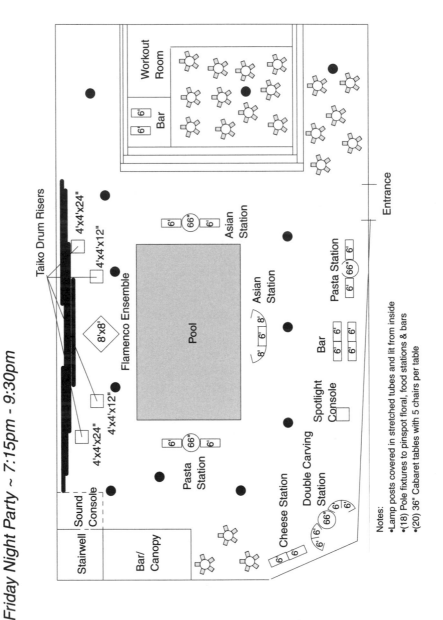

Reception
Hotel Pool Area
Friday Night Party ~ 7:15pm - 9:30pm

Notes:
•Lamp posts covered in stretched tubes and lit from inside
•(18) Pole fixtures to pinspot floral, food stations & bars
•(20) 36" Cabaret tables with 5 chairs per table

Staffing

Staffing Instructions

Spotter

- Spotters are stationed around the site to help guests find their way. You are also there to have answers regarding the grand opening.
- An employee (in a purple shirt) will be with you to answer specific questions regarding the site.
- All spotters move to production crew at 7:00 P.M. to assist with setting up the show site.
- All spotters then become people movers at 8:00 P.M. inside the site.
- If you have a problem, go to JK.
- If you have a question, ask JK.
- When you move from one area to the next, check in with JK.

Registration

- Registration people check in guests using their section of the guest list.
- Guests are given three items: credential, redemption card, and site map.
- If a guest parked in our assigned lot on Ohio, make sure they get their parking ticket stamped.
- Most registration people will move to giveaways at 7:00 P.M.
- All registration people will become people movers at 8:00 P.M.
- Some registration people will then assist with registration load-out.
- If you have a problem, go to DB.
- If you have a question, ask DB.
- When you move from one area to the next, check in with DB.

PWEE Staff

JW Inside venue
PW Hotel reception/people moving
ML Hotel reception/transportation/people moving
JK Site setup and strike/people moving
DB Registration/giveaways/people moving
MB Hotel reception/giveaways/people moving
AL Registration/site setup and strike/people moving
CC Registration/giveaways/people moving

Note

Our most important job is to make sure that the guests are continually informed of where they are going and that they feel welcome. The client has the site covered, so we need to make sure that the guests know where to park, where to register, where to go for the show, when the site officially opens to the public, where to get their transport back to the hotel (V-VIPs), and timing of everything.

- **If you run into a security problem, find one of us on radio.**
- No gum chewing.
- Do not bunch together.
- Always smile, try to be helpful, get the answer if you do not have it—don't guess the answer.
- You should be done around 10:00 P.M.

Multiroom Staffing

Friday
10:00 A.M.   PW/AL arrive for sound and lighting setup

Saturday
9:00 A.M.   PW/JW/DB/AL/JK
11:00 A.M.   ML/MB
5:00 P.M.   Registration staff arrives

Setup

JW/DB	Food station design, linens, and floral
AL	Hospitality and dressing rooms
AL/JK	Signage
JK	Radios
ML	Stanchion off drum troupe area (24 × 24 feet) on terrace
ML/MB	Gift bags
PW	S&L
ML	S&L, registration table setup
PW/MB	Sound checks and lion ceremony rehearsal

Event

ML	Registration, valet, security, harp duet, and troubleshooting
JW	Unveiling ceremony on terrace, second shift of drum troupe
PW	Marty Robinson, all production and lion dotting ceremony
DB	Ramsey Lewis, mariachis, photographers, and videographer
AL	Mass ensemble, cellist, and Georgia Francis Strings
JK	Jellyeye and gospel choir
MB	Joe Vito, Johnny Frigo, lion dancers, and Ultimate Band; assist PW with ceremony

Operations

Grand Opening Decor Details

	Furniture	Floral	Linen Rentals	Venue
Dessert Room	One (1) Carved Wood Art Piece	Floral & Candles Groupings of Silk Shantung & Bamboo Lanterns	Four (4) 6' Buffet Linens and Table Runner Overlays Linen For 10 Cabaret Tables	2 - 6' Banquet Tables (Coffee Station) 2 - 6' Banquet Tables (Dessert Station) 10 - 36" Cabaret Tables 50 Chairs (Existing)
Lobby Lounge		Two (2) Major Floral Pieces For: Sushi (6' Banquet Behind Station) & Caviar (72" Round) Loose Flowers For Lobster (72" Round) Floral & Votives For 12 Guest Tables	Two (2) Custom Brocade Linens with Red Crystal Beading (Lobster & Caviar) Two (2) 6' Serpentines With Lobster Display Runner for Prep Hutches (Lobster) Five (5) 6' Buffet Linens (Sushi Station) No Linens On The Guest Tables	2 - 72" Rounds (Existing) 2 - 6' Serpentine Tables 2 - Hutches for Prep (Existing) 5 - 6' Banquet Tables
Ballroom	Two (2) Asian Drums	12 Stainless Steel Buffet Tables: Center Buffet (Reflecting Pool) Major Floral On The Buffets One Major Piece In The Center Of The Reflecting Pool Buffet	Linen For 14 - 36" Cabaret Tables Linen For Two (2) Serpentine Tables (Corner Buffet)	14 - 36" Cabaret Tables 2 - Serpentine Tables 70 Chairs (Existing)
Terrace	Two (2) Large Garden Urns Two (2) Metal & Glass Lanterns Six (6) Asian Screens	Floral & Candles For 14 - 36" Cabarets Two (2) Grand Profusion of Flowers Bamboo & Steel Grass For Urns Table Runners For Buffets As Overlays	Linens For Two (2) Buffets ~ 3 - 8' Banquet Tables Linen For 14 - 36" Cabaret Tables	14 - 36" Rounds 6 - 8' Banquet Tables 70 Gold Opera Chairs
Avenues		One (1) Floral Piece For Kitchen Ledge Two (2) Grand Profusion of Flowers (Oyster) Vases For Oyster Display (# TBD) Eight (8) Guest Tables (Existing Floral) Center Table (Existing Floral)	2 - 6' Buffets	2 - 6' Banquet Tables
Spa		Candles For Pool (Number TBD)		
Suite		One (1) Tall Floral Piece		
Lower Lobby		Three (3) Registration Display Pieces	Four (4) 8' Registration Tables	4 - 8' Banquet Tables
Miscellaneous		40 Yellow Rose Boutonnières Loose Floral For Chef To Accent Trays, Etc. (Delivery 9 19.01)		1 - 12' x 12' Dance Floor (Terrace) 1 - 16' x 12' Dance Floor (Ballroom) 1 - 16' x 12' x 32' Stage (Terrace)

Power Requirements

Sound, Lighting, and Video

Gala (west lobby), 1-400 amp 3 phase for lighting, 1-100 amp
   3 phase for audio, 1-100 amp 3 phase for video

Dedication (outside facility), 1-100 amp single phase for audio, 1-200 amp
   3 phase for lighting

All other events (second-floor lobby), 2-100 amp single phase

All other events (third-floor lobby), 2-100 amp single phase

Catering

(2) 110 V, 15 amps for ovens
(8) 110 V regular outlets for coffee makers (must be separate outlets)

PWEE Radio Sign-In /Out

Serial Number	Company	Name	Received
6445			
7002			
7006			
7020			
7025			
7034			
7039			
7044			
7045			
7063			
7066			
7072			
7073			
7078			
7081			
7089			
7103			
7105			
7121			
7122			
7124			
7131			
7161			
7163			
7164			
7167			
7168			
7172			
7188			
7198			

Load-In/Load-Out

Load-In/Load-Out Schedule

Wednesday

10:00 A.M.   Load in staging

11:00 A.M.   Load in sound equipment

12:00 P.M.   Load in backline equipment

12:15 P.M.   Load in choral risers

12:30 P.M.   A/V loads in

1:30 P.M.   Atmosphere lighting loads in

2:30 P.M.   Designer loads in steel tables (ballroom)
Production meeting with Kate

3:30 P.M.   MDK's interviews

4:00 P.M.   Movers deliver food station decor to ballroom

5:00 P.M.   Sound picks up cases that cannot be stored in ballroom
Overnight security in place in ballroom

Thursday

9:00 A.M.   Designer loads in

10:00 A.M.   Load in grand piano (beautiful sounds)
Lighting continues setup

11:00 A.M.   Rentals load in
Lobby lounge setup begins

12:00 P.M.   Ceremony rehearsal in ballroom
Linens load in
Mass ensemble loads in (prefunction area on 6)
Hotel sets up hospitality in sixth floor hospitality room

2:00 P.M.   Ultimate band loads in (ballroom)

2:30 P.M.   Alex Fox loads in (roof terrace)
             Ultimate band sound check (until 3:30 P.M.)

3:00 P.M.   Mass ensemble sound check (until 4:00 P.M.)
             Alex Fox sound check (until 4:00 P.M.)

4:00 P.M.   Jellyeye loads in (roof terrace)
             Ramsey Lewis sound check (until 5:00 P.M.)

4:15 P.M.   Jellyeye sound check (until 5:00 P.M.)

4:45 P.M.   Choir checks in

5:00 P.M.   Focus lighting
             Choir sound check (until 5:45 P.M.)
             Hotel to set up (4) 8-foot registration tables with 12 chairs in lower lobby

5:30 P.M.   Harp duo loads in (lower lobby)
             String quartet loads in (lobby balcony)
             Joe Vito and John Frigo load in (pen bar)
             Valet arrives
             Security arrives
             Photographer arrives
             Videographer arrives
             Valet in place
             Registration staff in place

5:45 P.M.   Harp duo sound check (until 6:15 P.M.)
             String quartet sound check (until 6:15 P.M.)
             Joe Vito and John Frigo sound check (until 6:15 P.M.)
             Security in place
             Coat check, bathroom, and elevator attendants in place

6:00 P.M.   Floral Designer lights candles for pool display

6:30 P.M.   Event begins
             Bars and food stations open throughout hotel

187

6:30 P.M.	Georgia Frances String Quartet performs on lobby balcony (until 7:45 P.M.)
(cont.)	Harp duo performs in lower lobby (until 8:30 P.M.)
	Taped music in spa (until 11:00 P.M.)
	Pianist in suite (until 11:00 P.M.)

6:45 P.M.   Jellyeye to roof terrace (7 minutes)

7:00 P.M.   Mass ensemble to prefunction area (until 7:30 P.M.)
Joe Vito and John Frigo to bar (until 7:45 P.M.)
Chinese Dragon arrives
Alex Fox to roof terrace (until 7:45 P.M.)

7:30 P.M.   Mariachi band arrives

7:45 P.M.   Chicago Praise Choir performs in lobby lounge (until 8:00 P.M.)
Ramsey Lewis performs in ballroom (until 8:30 P.M.)
Cellist performs in prefunction area (until 8:15 P.M.)

7:55 P.M.   Ju Ming unveiling on terrace, Jellyeye performs immediately following

8:00 P.M.   Mariachi band to lobby lounge (until 8:30 P.M.)
Jellyeye to roof terrace (9 minutes)

8:15 P.M.   Joe Vito and John Frigo to pen bar (until 9:00 P.M.)

8:30 P.M.   One (1) registration table switches to giveaways
Mass ensemble to prefunction area (until 9:00 P.M.)
Georgia Frances String Quartet to lobby balcony (until 9:15 P.M.)
Alex Fox to roof terrace (until 9:30 P.M.)
Mariachis to ballroom (until 9:00 P.M.)

9:00 P.M.   Ramsey Lewis to ballroom (until 9:45 P.M.)

9:15 P.M.   Chicago Praise Choir to lobby lounge (until 9:30 P.M.)
Cellist to prefunction area (until 9:45 P.M.)

9:30 P.M.   Mariachi band to lobby lounge (until 10:00 P.M.)
Joe Vito and John Frigo to pen bar (until 10:15 P.M.)

188

9:45 P.M.	Jellyeye to roof terrace (6 minutes)
	Ultimate Band to ballroom (until 11:00 P.M.)
10:00 P.M.	Mass ensemble to prefunction area (until 10:30 P.M.)
	Georgia Frances String Quartet to lobby balcony (until 11:00 P.M.)
	Alex Fox to roof terrace (until 11:00 P.M.)
11:00 P.M.	Event ends; load-out begins
	Rentals load-out
	Jellyeye loads out drums
	Linens load out

Friday

12:00 A.M.	Load out floral and steel tables
	Load out backline equipment
12:15 A.M.	Load out grand piano
12:45 A.M.	Mass ensemble loads out long bow
	Load out sound equipment
1:45 A.M.	Load out staging
2:15 A.M.	Load out choral risers
9:00 A.M.	Pick up food station decor from ballroom
10:00 A.M.	Lighting equipment loads out

189

Financials

Estimated Budget (Based on 500 Guests)

Venue		<u>$39,000.00</u>
Venue fee	$25,585.00	
Bar package (includes tax and gratuity)	$13,415.00	
Food and Beverage		<u>$172,695.40</u>
Food stations and passed hors d'oeuvres	$37,500.00	
Food and beverage (provided by client)	$125,000.00	
Rentals (buffets and bars)	$5,195.40	
Chairs and cabaret tables (if needed)	$5,000.00	
Entertainment hospitality	Included	
Entertainment		<u>$131,950.00</u>
Name talent ~ delivered (includes 10 airfares)	$75,000.00	
Blues group	$3,500.00	
Game show	$2,500.00	
Game show prizes (including round trip package to Borgata)	TBD	
Human decor	$3,500.00	
Drum troupe	$5,500.00	
Ultimate band	$7,500.00	
Mass ensemble	$6,000.00	
Mariachi band (Provided by Client)	$6,900.00	
Mariachi band expenses	$5,100.00	
Gospel choir ~ 30 people	$5,000.00	
Chinese lion dancers	$3,500.00	
String quartet	$2,000.00	
Incidental talent	$2,750.00	
Harpists	$700.00	
Emcee	$2,500.00	
Production		<u>$29,000.00</u>
Ground, hospitality and misc. rider requirements*	$11,000.00	
Hotel accommodations	$10,000.00	
Augmented sound	$5,500.00	
Backline equipment	$2,500.00	

Décor		$36,218.61
Food stations linens	$2,025.01	
Food station decor	$4,193.60	
Shipping for food station decor	$1,000.00	
Floral for gallery	$4,000.00	
Food station and cocktail table floral	$12,500.00	
Candle display in pool	Included	
Lighting designer	$2,500.00	
Atmosphere and entertainment lighting	$10,000.00	
Printed Materials		$19,134.25
Save-the-date cards	Provided by client	
Invitations	$3,641.00	
Invitation design and samples	$3,940.00	
Calligraphy addressing	$4,733.25	
Estimated postage (based on 1,578)	$1,020.00	
Event schedule	$3,500.00	
Credentials (600)	$1,800.00	
Signage	$500.00	
Miscellaneous		$17,030.00
Rentals	$500.00	
Communications	$1,000.00	
Giveaways (600)	$6,000.00	
Photographer	$1,000.00	
Videographer	$2,500.00	
Estimated video edit	$750.00	
Blueprints	$1,200.00	
Valet parking (based on 150 cars)	$4,080.00	

191

Total		$445,028.26

* This includes in-house sound, lighting, stage manager, sound tech, and security.

Additional

Wedding Things to Do

Save-the-date
- ❏ Complete address list
- ❏ Review completed list with bride and groom
- ❏ Complete mailing
- ❏ Follow up with on response cards

Invitations
- ❏ Order by 10/20 (300 total)
- ❏ Complete charitable donation card by 10/25
- ❏ Hire calligrapher
- ❏ Other printing
- ❏ Wedding menu
- ❏ Table cards
- ❏ Ceremony program
- ❏ Dessert reception invite sent with wedding invitation
- ❏ Rehearsal dinner invite sent with wedding invitation

Hotels
- ❏ Complete by 10/25
- ❏ Drop off contract at Fitzpatrick Hotel
- ❏ Comprehensive hotel list of names, confirmation numbers, etc.
- ❏ Send hotel list to mother of bride
- ❏ Get contracts in order
- ❏ Confirm reservations for bride's family
- ❏ Reserve rooms for groom's family

192

Venue
- ❏ Timing for tasting
- ❏ Layout (PWEE)
- ❏ Traffic flow (PWEE)
- ❏ Photography setup
- ❏ Dinner layout (PWEE)
- ❏ Seating plan (MB/WW)
- ❏ Event timeline (PWEE)
- ❏ When to have strings play? (ceremony, cocktails, dinner?)

- ❏ Determine technical requirements for all music, speeches, etc. (PWEE)
- ❏ Source a sound and lighting company (PWEE)
- ❏ Need music list for band (PWEE)
- ❏ Pick songs (MB/WW)

Rehearsal dinner
- ❏ Food and beverage (PWEE)
- ❏ Tasting
- ❏ Finalize invitation list (MB/WW)
- ❏ Site survey (PWEE)
- ❏ Transportation to the venue
- ❏ Music (PWEE)
- ❏ Floral proposal

Dessert reception
- ❏ Food and beverage
- ❏ Tasting
- ❏ Layout
- ❏ Music?
- ❏ Floral proposal

Sunday brunch?
- ❏ Pick location
- ❏ Food and beverage
- ❏ Deposit
- ❏ Timing

Ceremony
- ❏ Secure rabbi
- ❏ Cancel central synagogue hold
- ❏ Get marriage certificate (blood tests?)
- ❏ Secure katubah (from rabbi?)
- ❏ Choose best man
- ❏ Write vows (you know who)
- ❏ Decide whether or not to have readings; if yes, who and what?
- ❏ Pick ring bearer
- ❏ Chuppa layout
- ❏ Usher configuration
- ❏ Determine technical requirements (video, sound, lighting, etc.)

193

❑ Pick music (MB/WW)
❑ Equipment rental (PWEE)

Floral
❑ Color coordinate bridesmaids' shawls with flowers
❑ Review candle concept with Preston
❑ Review lighting plan with Preston (PWEE)
❑ Secure initial design for Metropolitan from Preston (by 7/3)
❑ Decide on chuppa style and look

Photographer
❑ Meet with photographer (Chicago) in late August
❑ Photographer to provide videographer?
❑ Need photos in black and white, as well as in color

Wedding cake(s)
❑ Meet with cake designer (MAB/WEW/PWEE)
❑ Decide cake style
❑ Decide on individual wedding cakes
❑ Get proposal

Gifts
❑ Bridesmaids and maid of honor
❑ Bridesmaids shower
❑ Family shower
❑ Ushers and best man

194

Clothing
❑ Bridesmaids, shawls?
❑ Mother of bride dress
❑ Mother of groom dress
❑ Rehearsal dinner dress
❑ Baby outfit for
❑ Dye shoes for wedding

Hair/makeup
❑ Secure hair dresser for wedding party
❑ Secure dresser for bride (PWEE)
❑ Review makeup plan with cosmetic person
❑ Secure rooms for hair dressing and makeup

Appendix B:
List of Terms and Phrases

As with most industries, a certain common language develops over time, where those in the know can follow along and those outside can't. It's all meant to make working together easier, but inevitably, the novice ends up feeling left out. To avoid this, we've put together a list of the most common words and phrases we use daily, as well as how to use them.

We've found that a lot of these terms are very ordinary but used improperly and the meaning is lost. We're hoping that if you can throw a few of these around (in the right way, at the right time, and with the right people), you'll come off like a pro.

Jargon, Lingo, Slang, and Vernacular

Additionally insured   Used on certificates of insurance. You want to be named *additionally insured* on your vendor's insurance. Then you'll want a copy of that certificate naming you for your event book.

Atmosphere lighting   There are four main kinds of lighting: stage, general area, pin spotting, and atmosphere. Atmosphere lighting is categorized as decor. It is used to enhance the space as either a color wash on the walls or patterns on the floor, ceiling, or walls; you can highlight the outdoors by throwing light on trees or architectural elements of a building.

Attendants   There are all sorts of attendants. Valet attendants, coat check attendants, bathroom attendants, and elevator attendants. For almost any situation, you can have an attendant.

Back bar If your bars are made from banquet tables, most likely you'll need to also rent an additional table to be used as a *back bar*. The back bar is set up directly behind the bar that your guests approach and is used as a prep area for glassware, mixes, liquor, and so on.

Backdrop/stage set   Most people like to have some sort of decorative element behind their stage. It can be almost anything, but when discussing it with your sound and lighting people or your talent, you'll want to refer to it as the *backdrop*. If you have a backdrop behind the stage, as well as some decor on the stage itself, then you'll refer to all of these things together as the *stage set*.

Backline   Backline equipment is for entertainment. You usually only need it for name talent, but for that rare occasion when a local group requests it, you should know what they're asking for and what you're paying for. Backline equipment is rented instruments (and amps) for your band. They are most often pianos, drum kits, keyboards, or amplifiers. The band's *rider* will specify what their requirements are.

Bar package   A bar package is a set price based on the number of guests and is calculated per person per hour. The budget line item for drinks is set no matter how much liquor is consumed.

Call time   This term is used for everyone from labor crews to talent to staff. It's simply the arrival time that each person is to check in by.

Calligraphy   Everyone has heard of calligraphy, but while *hand calligraphy* can be expensive, there is a more cost-effective solution. *Computer calligraphy* is an option that some calligraphers offer.

Capacity   Depending on your event, the *capacity* of a space will change. Reception style will have a higher capacity than sit-down style.

Cash bar   When guests are asked to pay for their own drinks, it's called a *cash bar*.

Chairs (chivari, opera, wood padded, garden, etc.)   Chair names vary from region to region. Make sure that you see a picture or the actual chair that you are going to rent. An opera chair in one city may be called something different in another city.

Container   Whatever your floral arrangement is in is called the *container*. Sometimes it's a vase, sometimes an urn, and sometimes a pot. In any case, this general term covers all the above.

Corkage fee   If you were to provide your own wine or champagne, you most like would be charged a *corkage fee* per bottle opened.

Credentials   This is another general term to cover whatever process you've chosen to distinguish people who belong at your event versus those who do not. *Credential* styles can vary, and they're not just for guests.

Cutting fee   If you were to provide your own cake (be it wedding or otherwise), you most likely would need to get approval, and then you most likely would be charged a per-person *cutting fee*.

Decor   We don't use the word decorations (that's a little bit like a high school prom); we call it *decor*. And as we discussed in earlier chapters, decor is everything from lighting, to fabric, to linens, to food, to floral design, to as far as your creativity can be stretched.

Entertainment   *(incidental, interactive, name)* You can either use the blanket term *entertainment*, or if you want to be specific, you can use *incidental, interactive, local,* or *name* to alleviate some confusion.

Equipment   This term is used by your rental company (tables, chairs, etc.), by your sound and lighting company (speakers, monitors, lighting, etc.), and by your caterer (tables, caves, place settings, etc.).

Escort cards   *Escort cards* have a guest name on them with the table number to which that guest is assigned. You also should see *Place cards* and *Table cards*.

Event book   This is your organized book that has all the information for the event in it. This book rarely goes to the site with you (you should use a copy of your staff packet instead), or if you do bring it, leave it in your car, or in another safe place.

Event timeline   Different from the project timeline, your *event timeline* is a minute-by-minute account of what is going to happen at your party. Copies of this should be given to your vendors for reference, as well as the venue contact person.

Fabric   Used as a decor term, *fabric* is great for hiding things, covering things, and generally sprucing up a bland space.

Filler   This is a floral term. *Filler* can be a less expensive flower (sometimes the weedy looking ones) or greens.

Floor plans   The layout of your party (tables, chairs, stage, etc.) is referred to as the *floor plan*. This term usually is used when you're discussing an indoor event.

Floral (in season, local, and import)   We like to use this when we are talking about the general plan for all the *floral* arrangements. This term is used when we need to encompass the whole plan, which can include arrangements such as the entrance piece, the centerpieces, the bouquets, and so on.

Floral designer   Designer, *not* florist. There is a difference, and if you're working with someone who is very good at what she does, she is a *floral designer*.

Food & Beverage   Use *food and beverage* whenever you're referring to the menu for your party.

Fulfillment   When you stuff giveaway bags or assemble invitations, the service is called *fulfillment*.

Gobo   This is a lighting term for the metal plate that goes over a light and can shine shapes, words, or patterns. A lot of people have *custom gobos* made specifically for their event.

Hand verify   This is what we like to request of the post office when we're sending out very high-end printed materials. Most mail is verified via a machine, and that process can dirty the envelope, curl the edges, or even rip the paper. If the mail is *hand verified*, then these types of things can be avoided.

198   *Hospitality*   When you hire entertainment, from a tarot card reader to Madonna, they all will ask for *hospitality*. Depending on the talent, it can be simply soft drinks and water, or the hospitality request may be as much as dinner for 20, snacks in dressing rooms, bottles of champagne, and cases of water at the stage.

Hosted bar   Bars at events normally are paid for by the person/company hosting the event. This is referred to as a *hosted bar* with the drinks being complimentary to the guests.

Keystone   When you're doing projection you will need to correct the screen image so it isn't *keystoning*. This happens when the image is either wider or narrower at the top or bottom, or the same from side to side. Also see *Throw*.

Labor   This term can be used when discussing the budget, as in your *labor costs*. Or it can be used when discussing call times, as in your *labor call*. In either case, you're talking about the crew for a specific vendor or all the labor costs for the entire event.

Lighting   We use this term in reference to talent *lighting requirements* or our *lighting design*. In the first situation, you're referring to the stage lighting; in the second situation, you're referring to the decor of the space with regard to lighting.

Linens   Custom, rented, or purchased, all the fabric for your tables are referred to as *linens*.

Load-in/load-out   When you coordinate with your vendors and entertainment for their arrival times, setup times, tear-down times, and completion times, the whole process is called the *load-in/load-out*.

Logistics   Quite honestly, *logistics* is a nice way to talk about the challenges, issues, problems, and concerns in the successful execution of your event.

Menu planning   While *food and beverage* is a term used to talk about that element of your event, *menu planning* is the process by which you determine your food and beverage. *Menu planning* encompasses not only what you'll serve, but also how you'll serve it and what it will be served on.

Merge and purge   Some vendors offer this *merge and purge* service, which is so helpful when dealing with large-scale special events. For example, if you have two or more guest lists with addresses (say, for 1,000 people), you can have your lists merged together and then purged of any duplicates.

On consumption   One of three ways to pay for your bar, *on consumption* is based on how much your guests drink, usually with a minimum and is accompanied by a bartender fee.

199

Operations   Logistics and *operations* sometimes can be used interchangeably; most times they're used together. But essentially the difference is that logistics is used as a specific term for issues, and operations is a general term used for the overall event. For example, the operations for an event will include entertainment production, menu planning, decor design, and load-in/load-out. The logistics for an event will include the timing for load-in/load-out, where trucks will deliver product, and what elevator will be dedicated for the guests.

Overlays   This is a linen decor term for the linen that goes over the underlay. *Overlays* come in matching-size rounds or 84- or 96-inch squares.

Place cards   Place cards are at each place setting, letting your guests know the chair in which they are to sit. You also should see *escort cards* and *table cards.*

Power   This can be either a line item in your budget (charged to you by the venue) or the *power requirements* for your sound, lighting, or catering equipment. Power requirements usually are referred to in amps and circuits. Sound is always on a separate circuit from lighting (the lights cause a hum in your speakers), and caterers usually need power for their coffee makers.

Premium bar   Of the three type of bars, *well, standard,* and *premium*, premium is the most expensive. While the standard bar has all the same types of liquor, the premium bar is just that—the high-end versions of vodka, gin, tequila, rum, and so on.

Production   When you say *production,* you can be talking either about the production of the event or about entertainment production. Event production refers to the process of putting together the party, whereas entertainment production in your budget includes sound, staging, lighting, labor, airfares, ground transportation, hotel accommodations, and hospitality. You also can say *entertainment production* as in the process of coordinating all the items from your budget with regard to the talent.

Program   This is either the *program* for the event, such as speeches or performances, or it's the *event program* printed and distributed to your guests at the event.

Project timeline   As opposed to the *event timeline*, your *project timeline* encompasses the many weeks and months prior to the event. The project timeline consists of all your and your vendors' deadlines.

200   *Rehearsals*   Talent aren't the only people who need *rehearsals*. If you have speakers, they'll need to rehearse as well. Allot plenty of time in your load-in/load-out schedule for all rehearsals, and while your speakers rehearse, make sure that they know to keep the microphone at their chins for clarity.

Rentals   Tables, chairs, coat racks, warming caves, flatware, place settings, glassware, and even more are included in your *rentals*. The only thing that's separate is your linen rentals. Linens usually come from a different rental company.

Rider   When working with name talent, as part of the contract there will be a *rider*. In the rider the act will require all sorts of things from food to videos to flowers or clothes. As purchaser, you are required to provide these things.

Setup/tear-down   Once your vendors *load in*, they set up. And before they *load out*, they *tear down*. Each part takes time; make sure that you know the total amount of time they need to maintain an accurate load-in/load-out schedule.

Signage   *Signage* is much more than the banner at the front entrance. It's directional (as in which way to go); it's at your registration table (we split up the tables alphabetically); it's at valet (pickup and drop-off); it's on office doors, dressing room doors, and the food stations to label dishes; and it's essential at events, especially large ones. We try to source all our *signage* for a single event through a single vendor. When you put together your signage needs, don't forget to consider how the signage will be displayed. Will you put it on easels? Will you attach it with double-sided tape? Put it in a frame? Attach it to a post?

Site plans   While *floor plans* are usually for an indoor space, *site plans* are usually for an outdoor space. We also say site plans when we have multiple spaces or multiple floor plans. They are somewhat interchangeable, but it's better to understand the nuances.

Site lines   If you have a show or a program, you'll need to check your *site lines* for your guests. If your guests are at rounds and you have centerpieces, check the height of your floral to make sure that everyone, down to the last table in the back, can see the stage or screens. If you have theater style seating you'll want to do the same thing.

Sound & Lighting   When you have entertainment, you have *sound and lighting requirements* and will be working with either the audiovisual department at the venue, or you will be working with a *sound and lighting company*. Along with sound and lighting, you'll most likely be providing staging, you'll also be paying for power (whether your venue has it or you have to rent generators), and you'll also be responsible for the *labor* needed to *load in, set up, run, tear down,* and *load out* the *equipment*.

Sourcing   Searching for vendors or products is called *sourcing*.

Staff Handbook   These are the essential papers that contain all the information that your staff might need on site.

Standard bar   The moderately priced option to the *premium bar*, the *standard bar* provides all your liquor (standard brands), mixes, and juices. Standard bars also include beer, wine, soft drinks, and water.

Swagging   This is a general linen term used when you drape, tie, puddle, or pin fabric; either on tables, up on walls, or to make walls, and so on.

201

Table cards   *Table cards* are large numbers on each table so that guests know where to go for their seat (this number should be removed once everyone is seated). You also should see *escort cards* and *place cards*.

Tables (rounds and banquets)   The word *table* in the events business is not descriptive enough. Whether you're describing guest tables, cocktail tables, food stations, or buffets, you'll need to refer to each as either a round (preceded by the size in inches) or a banquet (preceded by the size in feet).

Taxable gratuity   In some states, the gratuity paid to a caterer or a hotel is taxable. Simply adding the percentages for tax and gratuity will net you an incorrect total. You first have to add in your gratuity and then tax the entire amount. Don't forget to ask your vendor or venue.

Technical requirements   This is strictly for when you're dealing with sound and lighting. For example, if you are to provide the sound and lighting for a band, you'll need to ask the band for its *technical requirements* and then forward those requirements to whomever is providing you with your equipment and labor.

Throw   When you talk about the *throw*, you're either referring to a light source or projection. For example, if you are lighting a floral piece, you'll want a light source that is adequate and close enough to have enough throw to sufficiently highlight the piece. When you do projection, the word *throw* refers to the distance of the image you are projecting. Thus, depending on the size of your space and the distance from the screen to your projector, you will need equipment with ample throw. Also see *Keystone*.

Vendor   For some unknown reason, in this industry we use the word *vendor* rather than supplier or subcontractor. It's just the way it is.

202

Venue   The *venue* is the location of your event. A venue can be anything from the convention center to the beach. When referring to your event location, you'll call it a *venue*.

Venue hold   If your venue is one of a more traditional nature (hotel ballroom, restaurant, museum, etc.), you'll initially put a *hold* on the space or more than one space. Eventually, you'll make a decision and then go to contract on your chosen space and then release the *hold* on the other venues.

Waitstaff   If you're talking to your caterer or banquet manager, you're going to be discussing their waitstaff. You'll be asking about how many there will be in *waitstaff* and where your *waitstaff* will be stationed.

Wash   We use this term primarily when we're talking about lighting for a stage. When we're not doing something great with lighting for a stage or maybe it's just some background music type of band, then we ask for a *stage wash*. This typically includes a limited number of *cans*, not intelligent, lighting with some color to light the band but not necessarily highlight the band.

Well bar   Of the three types of bars, the *well bar*, consisting of well liquor, beer, wine, and soft drinks, is the least expensive package including liquor.

Understanding Common Phrases

> *"I want to drop the 120s on all the rounds, including the pedestal 36s which we're going to tie because of the wind. Otherwise use the 96s on the indoor cocktails. Then we have banquets for the 6-foot's and the 8-foot's, but we're swagging the overlay to the front center point."*

> *"We really should fly the sound to have better sightlines and so we don't blast the front tables with the speaker stacks."*

Having the right words can be different from stringing them together to make sense. We've split up the most common phrases and the translations into different event elements so that it's easier to follow along.

Decor

Linens

Linens are *dropped,* and they can be *swagged.* When you rent linens for your guest tables and food stations, placing them on the tables is called *dropping linens*. If you have an overlay or need to pin up the linens, you're *swagging* them.

Linens also come in sizes referred to in inches. So the most common sizes are 132 inches (for a 72-inch round), 120 inches (for a 60-inch round), 96 inches (for a 36-inch round), 90 inches (for 30-inch round), overlay squares that are either 84 or 96 inches, and banquet linens for either a 6- or 8-foot table.

So the phrase above is stating that we're placing the 120-inch round linens on the 60-inch tables, as well as the smaller 36-inch cocktail table pedestal legs, but we're tying the linens around the cocktail tables to keep the wind from blowing them. For the indoor cocktails tables, we're using the standard 96-inch round linens and letting them drape to the floor. On the food stations, which are a combination of 6- and 8-foot banquet tables, we are placing corresponding linens on them, but there are square overlays that will be placed on top, with the corner of the squares centered and draped over the front of the table.

Floral

When you're buying your floral arrangements, the most common pieces you'll have are the *centerpieces*. Everyone pretty much knows this, but to describe the style of the centerpiece is a little different. A tightly assembled arrangement can be described as *pavé*. If you're looking for a lot of pastel colors, you're looking for a *spring arrangement;* if you want the deep reds and oranges, you're looking for *jewel tones;* if you prefer a lot of greens or grasses, those are called *filler*. The vase is usually referred to as the *container*. When you sit down with your floral designer (not florist), you would say, "My favorite look is a low, pave piece, jewel-toned floral with little to no greens or filler." Or if your event is during the day and outside, maybe you would say, "I would like a fresh spring look, loose arrangement in a casual container."

Equipment Rental

Chairs

When hosting an event in a hotel, the hotel has *in-house chairs*. There isn't usually a rental fee associated with using the hotel chairs unless the hotel keeps certain types in storage specifically for rental. Rental chairs come in several different types. The most common are the *Chivari* (bamboo-like backs and legs, used for more high-end events), the *opera* (a wood chair that is curved at the back and comfortable, also used at high-end events), *wood-padded chair* (folding chair, most common chair rented), and the *garden chair* or *Samsonite chair* (plastic chair, reserved for more casual events). The first three chairs come in different colors, with the option for different colors for the pads or even custom pads. The garden chair is the least expensive, but it is also the least comfortable and not the nicest. Garden chairs usually come in an off-white color. Thus, if you were doing a wedding at a hotel, you probably would request to use the in-house chairs for the dinner and then rent white or natural wood-padded chairs for the ceremony if it's outside or maybe the opera or Chivari chairs if the ceremony is inside. A typical order may sound like this: "We're going to need 200 mahogany Chivaris with an ivory pad set up theater style on the lawn. For cocktails, we'll need 100 natural wood-padded chairs with an ivory cushion set up five around each 36-inch round and an extra five for the talent."

Tables

Tables can be just as complicated to order and rent. Tables are called *rounds* or *banquets*, and you must be very specific about what sizes you need. When you're renting tables, you'll want to say the size and type and number of tables you'll need. Therefore, rounds come in seven sizes, 72 inches (10 to 12 people), 60 inches (8 to 10 people), 54 inches (8 people), 48 inches (6 to 8 people), and 36 inches (4 to 5 people). The less common sizes are 66 inches (10 people) and 30 inches (4 people). Knowing the sizes of your tables is an essential piece of information, especially when you're doing your floor plan and renting your linens. Depending on where you live, some tables have names as well, and these names differ from one region to the next. The 36-inch round and the 30-inch round, at chair height, are sometimes called *cabaret tables* or *cocktail tables*. At stand-up height, they also can be called *hi-boys* or *belly bars*. To avoid confusion, you should call them by their size and height.

The other type of table you may be renting is the banquet table. These are simply the rectangular tables used for food stations, bars, registration tables, and guest tables. We follow the same rules for banquets as we do for rounds. Banquets are easier, though, because they come in two sizes (with a few exceptions), 6-foot banquets and 8-foot banquets. Notice that we've moved from inches to feet. If you're at a venue that provides food and beverage, most likely you won't need to rent banquets unless you're using them for guest tables. If you're working with a caterer, you may need to order the tables for the food stations and bars. The caterer will tell you how many he or she needs and in what sizes. When you place your order, you'll simply say: "I need *x* number of 6-foot banquets and *x* number of 8-foot banquets." If you've paid to have the rental company set up your tables, then you'll also provide them with a floor plan of where everything is placed.

Place Setting

Apart from the obvious, there are a few terms that we use when discussing the place setting. Depending on the number of guests per table and the size of your table, you may use a *charger*. Chargers are only possible for eight guests at 60- or 66-inch rounds or for ten people at a 72-inch round. There simply isn't enough space for everything at smaller tables. We also talk about the *b&b plate*—the bread and butter plate. We sometimes use these smaller plates for things other than the bread and butter. To cut down on rentals, we'll use them for candy display on the table. Lastly, you'll need to choose your napkin fold. Seems like a minute detail, but there are so many styles, and each fold can change the look of your place setting significantly. Some are simple (the tuxedo fold), some are elaborate (bird of paradise), some go in a wine glass, and sometimes you insert the menu card or a flower. Have an idea of what you think you want, and then request that the caterer or venue show you the different options.

Food and Beverage

Plated

We discussed the type of service in the food and beverage chapter, but you also have some other options to consider. One is a *preset course*. Usually reserved for the first course or the salad course, this is a good time saver. You'll need to decide if your bread is *set* at the table or *waiter offered* to each guest. Lastly, how are you to serve the coffee? Do you *set* your cups and saucers? Or do you have a waiter offer coffee to each guest with another waiter to follow filling each cup? As you choose your service, discuss with your vendor/venue about *clearing*, as well as how they're going to serve. You'll want to know if they bring in stacks of plates with silver trays on top, or do they have lots of staff and plates are brought out to each table individually.

Food Stations

When it comes to food stations, there are more decisions to make. Are your stations *double-sided* (guests can approach the table from both sides to serve themselves)? Are your stations *self-service,* or do you have a *chef carving* or a *waitstaff person serving*? Sometime they're a combination of both. We generally stick to *one-sided* food stations because double-sided ones tend to feel like a cafeteria. If your event is entirely reception style, then you'll need to decide when the *changeover* will happen, which is the move from main course to dessert. Also, which stations will change and which will remain? Thus, when we do food stations, we do *one-sided stations, duplicated to alleviate lines, with the stations open for service right away, and a dessert changeover approximately 90 minutes into the party*.

Talent

There are some universal terms we use whether we're *booking* (hiring) incidental entertainment all the way through to name talent. When you book talent, you'll ask them if the cost is their *fee plus, plus*. When you have a local dance band, for example, they'll charge you a fee to come perform, but you also may have to cover their parking, pay for their dinner (hospitality), and provide sound and lighting, or that all may be included in the price. When you're dealing with name talent, the performance fee is only that. You are also responsible for *production, airfares, ground transportation, hotel accommodations, hospitality,* and *possibly per diem.* If you're booking name talent for a private event, that is sometimes called a *one-off.* It's different in that your date is not part of a tour. Sometimes you can contract name talent to be *delivered* (which means that their airfares are included in the fee paid by you locked in at a mutually agreed upon number). Another term used is *doing the advance.* This is when the tour manager or band manager calls you to get the information on the venue, hotel, confirmation numbers, and so on. While these are common terms used in the world of name talent, we wouldn't necessarily recommend that the first-time buyer throw them around. It's easy to get caught in this industry, and if you're not totally confident in your knowledge, you can end up with egg on your face. Better to ask questions and work with your vendors than to look like an amateur.

Sound & Lighting

Sound

In the opening we talked about *flying the sound.* This means that the speakers are suspending from the ceiling (if it can withstand the load) instead of *stacking* the speakers on the corners of the stage. Flying sound is a good option for getting even coverage and not breaking the eardrums of the (inevitably) older groups at the tables that are placed right at the stage. When you begin working with your sound and lighting vendors, they'll use words like *monitors, soundboard, console board,* and *front of house.* Monitors are how the band hear themselves on stage. The soundboard or console board is how the sound technician manages the sound, and the front of house is where these controls boards are placed (usually directly opposite the stage in the venue).

Staging

Staging comes in platform sections, mostly in 4×4 foot or 4×8 foot sections. When you need staging, you'll refer to it in feet *and* inches. For a local dance band, as an example, for six musicians, you could use a 12-foot $\times$ 16-foot $\times$ 24-inch high stage. The height of the stage is always in inches, while the depth and width are always in feet. It's a mystery, but that's the way we all communicate. At private events, you'll rarely need a stage higher than 24 to 30 inches high. It just looks funny. The 60-inch-high stages usually are reserved for large concerts. Part of staging is the *drum riser.* This is just another section or more of *platform* set on top of the stage for the drum kit. So you know, most hotels keep an inventory of platforms, and they can set them up for you. If you're working with a sound and lighting company, they can coordinate that for you.

Lighting

Lighting is that forgotten element that can make an event. Most of our clients don't always see the benefit of a hefty lighting line item in their budget, but the right lighting on your stage, pin spotting your centerpieces, or throwing images on walls or ceilings can create a unique event. What's so incredible about great lighting is that the look of your event can change *during the course* of your event. Which brings us to the phrases for the *different looks* that you need to choose. When your stage or the general look of your event is the main element of your event, you'll work with your lighting designer (or *LD*) to choose your *walk-in look, walk-out look, dinner look,* and *speeches look* and then at what time all those looks will occur. As part of your *lighting design,* you may have *intelligent lights* (lights that move, project patterns, and change colors) as part of the equipment. If you do, then your LD will work with the different patterns and colors to create the looks for your event.

Index

211

215

Paulette Wolf, CEO

PAULETTE WOLF has been an innovator and leader in the event-management field for over 30 years. Originally an interior designer by trade, she loved parties and thought she could add some flair to uneventful soirees. Soon she was known for transforming staid cocktail parties into themed extravaganzas. One appreciative attendee, who happened to be a McDonald's franchise owner-operator, knew the parent company was looking to outsource a series of special events to celebrate its twentieth anniversary. He opened the door for Paulette and launched a decade of collaboration between her and the corporate giant.

Initially, Paulette serviced this major account through an established entertainment production company, personally handling all aspects of event management, including the hiring and producing of name talent such as Tina Turner, Kenny Loggins, and Jay Leno. In 1978, with McDonald's encouragement, she forged out on her own, forming Paulette Wolf Productions. She continued producing blowout events for her flagship account as well as for a growing list of blue-chip clientele.

Paulette's reputation continued to expand and soon found her managing high-profile, prestigious public events. By the mid-1990s (and one company name change to Paulette Wolf Events & Entertainment, Inc. [PWEE]), Paulette had secured a number of prominent events, including the 1996 Centennial Olympic Games, where the Olympic Committee enlisted her diverse skills to manage all production elements for six different entertainment venues located within the Athlete Village. Two hundred and fifty live acts and 33 days later, Paulette had put together an entertainment program for literally a worldwide audience of 16,000 people speaking over 100 different languages.

Today, Paulette and her team continue to produce events with the same vigor for clients such as "The Oprah Show," M&M Mars, Harley-Davidson Owner's Group, the Federal Reserve, and DIFFA.

Her creativity truly knows no boundaries.

Jodi Wolf, President

JODI WOLF is president of Paulette Wolf Events & Entertainment, Inc., a company formed in 1978 by her mother Paulette. Under her creative leadership, the company is retained by organizations nationally whose primary events usually involve multiple happenings, often in several cities, requiring contract negotiations, city services coordination, site logistics, crowd control, security, and complete entertainment production.

Jodi, who joined the company in 1993 as a production coordinator, was promoted to vice president in 1996 when she was key to securing the Summer Olympics project in Atlanta. She became president in May 2002, when the company expanded to include a Los Angeles office.

Freshly graduated from the University of Southern California, Jodi decided to cut her teeth in the events trade working for what would be considered vendor industries. She "paid her dues" at places such as the Hotel Sofitel in Los Angeles, Academy Tent & Canvas, and later Somerset Catering, before returning to Chicago.

Since becoming president, Jodi has sought to create an elevated standing for the firm, attracting the nation's largest corporations, municipalities, sporting events, and foundations. Shortly after assuming the presidency, she opened a satellite office in Los Angeles and is currently considering New York City, Las Vegas, and Miami, all cities where the firm does a significant amount of business annually.

Since 1995, Jodi has presided over such projects as the Ft. Lauderdale Air and Sea Show, the largest spectator event in the world, attracting four million people during its two-day run. Her dedication to the Disney brand from 1998 to today has garnered PWEE several projects, including multicity grand openings of ESPN Zone entertainment complexes and a DisneyQuest indoor interactive theme park, as well as several movie premieres across the country. Cultivating strong creative partnerships with a powerful roster of new and long-term clients continues to be both her primary focus and her reward.

Paulette Wolf Events & Entertainment, Inc.

Considered a pioneer in the development of professional event management, Paulette Wolf Events & Entertainment, Inc. (PWEE), had its start over 30 years ago. Known for unique creative development and originality, the company has grown to become one of the nation's most sought-after production firms.

In the arenas of sporting and corporate events, the company's design innovation and extensive expertise are unrivaled. Hired to produce the corporate hospitality area for Super Bowl XXI in Pasadena, California, PWEE refined the corporate hospitality concept with organizational efficiency. With PWEE's lead, this "village" concept has since become the prototype for most major sporting events today. PWEE then subsequently created and produced hospitality villages for world-class sporting events such as the Super Bowl, The U.S. Open Golf Championship, and the Kentucky Derby.

Since the close of the last century, PWEE has cultivated a new specialty of high-profile PR-driven events. Successful productions of groundbreakings, grand openings, product launches, and anniversaries have earned the firm loyal clients such as Northwestern Memorial Hospital, Urban Retail Group, William Blair & Company, and Masterfoods USA/M&M Mars.

A strong sense of community from the firm's inception has guaranteed PWEE's strong presence in the not-for-profit arena as well. From the Michael Jordan Foundation, the Elizabeth Taylor AIDS Foundation, and DIFFA to the creation of original fund-raising programming such as Equilibrium and H_2O—The Fire Hydrant Project, the PWEE team continues to serve the nonprofit sector with original events and campaigns nationally.

Paulette Wolf Events & Entertainment, Inc., is headquartered at 3300 W. Franklin Blvd., Chicago, IL 60624, and can be reached at (773) 475-4300 or at *www.paulettewolfevents.com.*

221

Top Venue Choices

Favorite Vendors

Favorite Entertainment

Clever Gift Ideas

Décor Ideas

Notes